THE INNER STAGE:

*An Essay on the Conflict of Vocations
in the Early Works of Paul Claudel*

Claudel at Twenty-one

THE INNER STAGE

An Essay on the Conflict of Vocations
in the Early Works of Paul Claudel

by

RICHARD BERCHAN

THE MICHIGAN STATE UNIVERSITY PRESS

1966

★
★
★
★
★

To *Mary* and *Monica*

Acknowledgments

I should like to thank *Gallimard* for permission to quote and translate passages from several works identified in my text and *Lettres Modernes* for permission to cite from Ernest Beaumont's *Le Sens de l'amour dans le théâtre de Claudel.* I am also grateful to Appleton-Century and to Louis Chaigne for permission to quote from his *Vie de Paul Claudel,* and to Henri Guillemin for allowing me to cite passages from his articles on Claudel which have appeared in the *Revue de Paris.* The *Société Paul Claudel* has also been gracious in consenting to the use of the photograph of Claudel appearing in this book.

No special claims are made for the translations of the French passages; they are there to assist the reader in his reading of the original. I am particularly grateful, however, to John Thompson for his invaluable assistance in the translation of the poetry. My colleague, Laurence Porter, was generous in his painstaking reading of the manuscript. I am indebted to him for his helpful suggestions.

Finally, I should like to thank Lyle Blair, Director of the Michigan State University Press, for making this book possible.

Mes drames n'ont jamais été pour moi que des engins plus ou moins compliqués destinés à l'épuisement de la conversation intérieure . . .

[My plays have never been anything but more or less elaborate devices to allow my inner debate to talk itself out . . .]

Letter from Claudel to Francis Jammes, August 12, 1900.

I. COLLECTIONS

OC	*Oeuvres complètes*
OP	*Oeuvre poétique*
Th. I	*Théâtre,* Vol. I
Th. II	*Théâtre,* Vol. II

II. INDIVIDUAL WORKS

La Ville II	*La Ville,* second version (1897)
Violaine	*La Jeune fille Violaine,* first version (1892)
Violaine II	*La Jeune fille Violaine,* second version, (1898)
Repos	*Le Repos du Septième Jour*
Partage	*Partage de Midi*

III. OTHER

AP	Angers, *Commentaire à l'Art Poétique de Paul Claudel, avec la texte de l'Art Poétique*
Bonnefoy, *Rimbaud*	Yves Bonnefoy, *Rimbaud par lui-même*
Cahiers I	*Cahiers Paul Claudel,* Vol. I
Cahiers IV	*Cahiers Paul Claudel,* Vol. IV
Corresp. Cl./Jam./Friz.	*Paul Claudel, Francis Jammes, Gabriel Frizeau: Correspondance (1897-1938)*
Corresp. Cl./Gide	*Paul Claudel et André Gide: Correspondance (1899-1926)*
Corresp. Cl./Riv.	*Jacques Rivière et Paul Claudel: Correspondance (1907-1914)*
Chaigne, *Vie*	Louis Chaigne, *Vie de Paul Claudel et genèse de son oeuvre*
EC	*Etudes Classiques*
Madaule, *Drame*	Jacques Madaule, *Le Drame de Paul Claudel*
MI	*Mémoires improvisés*
RP	*Revue de Paris*

CONTENTS

CHAPTER I

In Quest of Love:
From Vision to Reality

In 1886, Paul Claudel was seventeen years old. In that crowded and fateful year he discovered and was transfixed by the poetry of Rimbaud; he began writing his first play, a short pastoral farce on the theme of the Sleeping Beauty;[1] he experienced a religious "illumination" on Christmas day, during a visit to Notre-Dame, which led to his formal return to Catholicism four years later and eventually to an obsessive need to enter monastic life; finally, the artist in him had a sudden intuition of what his work must strive to express.

During the next twenty years, until his marriage in 1906 (which brings to a close the period of his early works) Claudel was torn by a dramatic conflict between his artistic and his religious vocations. This conflict fed on the contradictions of his character, on the clash in him of neopagan and mystical tendencies. It reached a critical turning point in the year 1900 with his unsuccessful attempt to renounce his art in favor of the priesthood.

All the plays and poetry composed during this period (from *L'Endormie* in 1886 to *Partage de Midi* in 1905) acquire their fullest meaning when studied chronologically in the light of the conflict of vocations. These works are the fruit of this conflict. As Claudel struggled to turn his back on his poetic gift, he evolved, in spite of himself, a poetic program which served as counterweight to what might be called his yearning for sainthood. In this poetic program—a compromise born of the instinct

1

of self-preservation—the poet-diplomat cast himself in the rôle of poet-priest to resolve the conflict of vocations; in effect, he appointed himself, in Robert Mallet's apt phrase, "Ambassador of God."[2]

Claudel had an irrepressible curiosity about the universe, akin to hunger, sustained by a powerful imagination and an unwavering faith in his own talent. At the same time, he had a child-like need to be loved, largely repressed by an uncompromising pride, as his family was undemonstrative and even sneeringly on the lookout for any form of adolescent sentimentality ("Our mother never kissed us" Claudel told Henri Guillemin).[3] Behind his urgent need for love was a haunting fear of death, sustained by his memory of the slow, agonizing death of his grandfather in September, 1881, which he had witnessed, and by his reading, at the age of sixteen, of Zola's *La Joie de Vivre*, a morbid study of a young man's unsuccessful battle with the fear of death.

Before Claudel discovered the works of Rimbaud, early in 1886, his sensibility must have already connected his need for love with his apprehension of death, to create the intuition that his love-quest was condemned to death, that human love was a pathetic comedy incapable of generating lasting joy. This is precisely what he found confirmed in Rimbaud. Behind Rimbaud's violent hatred of the threatening world he knew lay a metaphysical anguish rooted in a love-quest inseparable from the intuition of its doom. "Rimbaud never sought love without a premonition of failure," writes Yves Bonnefoy in *Rimbaud par lui-même*.[4] "To understand Rimbaud" he adds—in a statement which applies equally to Claudel—"one must go back to the teachings of Platonism and remember that a metaphysics of love which shows it to be instrumental in transcending the sensory world, in liberating man from exile, is not devoid of psychological truth and relates our individual existence to the larger concept of being" (*Rimbaud*, p. 17).

What drew Claudel to Rimbaud, as he read the opening poems of *Illuminations*,[5] was the sudden discovery of a kindred spirit in whom he recognized a metaphysical anxiety identical to his own. "Rimbaud will try to *re-invent love,* to *steal the fire,* thus embracing what I should like to call heroic causality . . ." (Bonnefoy, *Rimbaud,* p. 21). The encounter with Rimbaud represents a ray of hope in a desolate adolescence lifted suddenly out of its loneliness. Claudel will worship Rimbaud for the same reasons that Cébès worships Tête d'Or: to escape from self and to seek, in the footsteps of a spiritual brother, a remedy for the agony in his heart.

That agony is hidden in *L'Endormie.* This short pastoral farce is centered on a young poet in quest of love and on a mysterious nymph, Galaxaure, condemned to sleep until touched by a poet's message of love. Two mischievous fauns, Danse-la-Nuit and Volpilla, persuade the poet to attempt to awaken the nymph by the power of his verse. Confident that he has succeeded, he enters a grotto pointed out to him, but instead of the beautiful nymph he finds a drunken, monstrous female, Strombo, whom he had earlier pursued eagerly through the woods. Angry and bewildered, the poet understands too late that he is the victim of a prank. A group of passing fauns carry him away, to the great delight of his tormentors.

Thus summarized, this one-act pastoral, only sixteen pages long, may appear of little interest. However, a close look at the text uncovers complex motives behind the mystification inflicted upon the "poet," a grotesque figure sufficiently like the young Claudel to be a self-caricature. A clue to Claudel's motives is provided by Danse-la-Nuit's curious attitude towards the sleeping nymph: "Sleep," he exclaims, "sleep on, Galaxaure, Galaxaure the white, most beautiful of nymphs, my dearest, my beautiful! Sleep tight! You may sleep peacefully; the day has not yet come when you will awaken" (p. 6).

This curious interest in her fate later leads him to keep her imprisoned in sleep by mystifying her potential savior, the poet. He knows but does not reveal that wine-soaked Strombo (the only earthly woman in the play) has just fallen into the grotto

by accident, and deceitfully recites to the poet the moving story
of the nymph in order to induce him to act:

> *Son nom est Galaxaure.*
> *C'est une des nymphes de la mer dont les troupes*
>   *aux cheveux rouges dansent autour des*
>   *monstrueuses baleines*
> *Quand l'immense matin d'or court*
> *Sur l'Océan, traîné par les longues lames vertes!*
> *Mais un jour elle sortit de la mer et voulut*
> *Sécher sur le gazon son corps ruisselant de l'écume*
>   *salée,*
> *Et ici elle s'endormit en mordant doucement une*
>   *fleur, hélas!*
> *Hélas, cette fleur! ses soeurs les nymphes et son*
>   *père le vieux roi*
> *Qui siège dans les grottes pourpres de la mer*
> *Se sont souvent écrié: "O Galaxaure!*
> *Galaxaure la blanche, plût au ciel que tu ne*
>   *l'eusses pas mordue!"*
> *Car elle dort toujours avant qu'un poëte*
> *Par sa parole n'ait réussi à la réveiller.* (pp. 11-12)

> [Her name is Galaxaure.
> She is one of those red-haired sea nymphs who dance
>   in troupes around monstrous whales
> When the immense golden morning sweeps
> Over the ocean, drawn by long green waves!
> But one day she stepped from the sea and wished
> To dry her salt-foam-streaming body on the turf,
> And here she fell asleep, biting gently on a
>   flower, alas!
> Alas, that flower! Her sisters the nymphs and
>   her father the old king
> Enthroned in the purple grottoes of the sea
> Have often cried out: "O Galaxaure!

Galaxaure the white, would to heaven you had
    never bitten it!"
For she will sleep on until a poet succeeds, by
    his words, in reawakening her.]

In this sober recital—in sharp contrast with the Dionysian
atmosphere of the other faun scenes—Danse-la-Nuit plays an
ambiguous rôle. Though no mean poet—"I feel as comfortable
in my old body tonight as a peach conscious of growing ripe
[*Je suis aussi à mon aise ce soir dans mon vieux corps qu'une
pêche qui se sent mûrir*],"—he is unable to rouse the nymph
himself. Acting out of jealous possessiveness ("Oh! you are too
old to be jealous" his companion remarks in mock complaint,
p. 9), he makes sure that the poet too is frustrated in his attempt
to awaken Galaxaure, to bring to life the fiction of his erotic
imagination. In the wild closing scene of the play, the poet meets
not his dream, but its grotesque caricature:

*Une femme! ce n'est pas une femme, c'est une bedaine,
c'est un tonneau enterré dans le sable, une baleine pâmée,
une quille de navire retourné par le vent! Elle était vautrée
comme les vieux chevaux facétieux à qui le dos démange
en été et qui se roulent dans la poussière en gigotant lan-
guissamment. Quel monstre! Oh! quand je suis entré, son
ventre était balayé par les rayons de la lune, je le prenais
pour le sein d'une géante. Alors elle s'est éveillée et elle
s'est mise à bafouiller je ne sais quoi d'une voix plus
enrouée qu'un vieux canard, qu'un cornet de carnaval . . .*
(p. 17)

[A woman! This is not a woman, it is a paunch, a barrel
half-buried in the sand, a stranded whale, a ship's hull over-
turned by the wind. She was wallowing like a clownish flea-
bitten old nag whose back itches in summer and who rolls
in the dust, languidly kicking his legs. What a monster!
O! When I went in, the moonlight was sweeping over her

belly which I took for the breast of a giantess. Then she awoke and set to spluttering God knows what in a voice more grating than an old duck's—as hoarse as a fog-horn . . .]

The sadistic delight which the instigators of the deception exhibit, as they witness this confrontation of dream and reality ("Do you hear him? He screams like a woman being raped or like someone who inadvertently plunges his feet in boiling water" p. 17) suggests that in Claudel's mind nature, represented by these fauns, is aligned against man's dream of fulfillment through earthly love. The serious love-theme in the play is expressed through Danse-la-Nuit. Claudel has here contrived a curious *dédoublement*, motivated by timidity and wounded pride. Having no faith in the possible fulfillment of the love-quest, he creates with the character of the poet a grotesque caricature of his own yearning for love. But it is sufficiently transparent to betray the despair of his adolescent years, and indeed, the love fixation of his life.[6]

The most important insight into Claudel which *L'Endormie* affords is the symbolic link between Galaxaure and Strombo: they are both part of the same oneiric vision of love. Upon confrontation, Galaxaure, object of the poet's love-dream, emerges a horrible monster. The love-dream in the young Claudel is poisoned at the source, precisely as in Rimbaud. The play reveals a fundamental metaphysical anxiety in Claudel which accounts for its underlying bitterness. Its message seems to be that man, by the very nature of the human condition, is mystified, derided and humiliated in his need for love. Claudel's "illumination" by Rimbaud in May, 1886, and his conversion six months later represent, on the human plane at least, a groping desire to find a viable solution to this need for love.

On December 25, 1886, Claudel went to Notre-Dame de Paris with nothing more in mind, he thought, than to observe the service and perhaps to find inspiration for some "decadent" poetry. What actually happened on that fateful day, as he reconstructs it, is recorded in a now famous article entitled, "Ma Conversion," published for the first time in 1913 in the October 10 issue of *La Revue des jeunes:*[7]

> Suddenly my heart was touched and *I believed*. I believed so completely, with such total consent of my entire being, with so strong a conviction, leaving no room whatever for doubt, that since then all the books I have read, all the arguments and all the events encountered during a very active life have not been able to shake my faith, nor indeed even to touch it. I had suddenly had the heart-rending and ineffable revelation of the eternal, child-like innocence of God. (*OC*, XVI, 191)

Claudel recalls, in "*Ma Conversion*," the internal dialogue which attended this moment of revelation: "How happy are those who believe! What if it were true? *It is true!* God exists, He is there, a being as real as myself! He loves me, he is calling me" (pp. 191-192).

The bliss resulting from the sudden belief that God loved him, Paul Claudel,[8] and was calling him, parallels the hoped-for but frustrated *dénouement* of *L'Endormie*, granted here at the moment of belief. At the same time, however, Claudel recalled experiencing "a feeling of terror, almost of horror" which he attributed to the threat of the compelling experience of grace: "The edifice of my knowledge and opinions had not collapsed, nor did I find fault with it. I had merely moved out of it" (p. 192).

During the next four years, until his formal return to Catholicism in December, 1890, Claudel experienced a complicated inner conflict. He desperately wanted to preserve his new-found bliss (". . . what did the rest of the world matter to me next to this new and prodigious Being which had just been revealed to me?" p. 193). Simultaneously, he was mobilizing all his energies to reject it, in order to protect and preserve his threatened identity: "The condition of a man suddenly pulled out of his own skin and placed in an alien body somewhere in an unknown world is the only comparison I can find to describe my state of total bewilderment" (p. 192). With all his strength he resisted the menacing divine injunction: "I dare say I defended myself splendidly and loyally to the bitter end. Nothing was omitted. I used all conceivable means of resistance . . ." (p. 192). In this battle between spirit and intellect, candor and pride, between a highly vulnerable human being and a harsh, cynical, and callous world, Claudel's instinct of self-preservation found an ally in the atheistic naturalism of the day, with which he was in complete intellectual sympathy. To be sure, he was defending a world view that gave him no joy, that accentuated his private despair and that was gradually leading him into a moral and spiritual impasse.[9] Nevertheless, he had accepted his family's emancipation from religious practices and convictions, and even despised dogmas and priests alike: "Catholicism still seemed to me the same thesaurus of absurd tales, and its priests and faithful still revolted me to the point of hatred" (p. 192). It is no wonder that he viewed with apprehension the prospect of revealing his conversion at home ("The very thought of mentioning it . . . put me in a sweat . . ." p. 193), for the likelihood of public ridicule at the hands of a ferocious Claudel clan was more real than ever and had already threatened to give him an inferiority complex.[10]

But the most appalling prospect must have been the necessity of baring his soul to the very priests he detested, in order to enlist their help in destroying his own romantic posture. Up to his moment of bliss at Notre-Dame, his deepest affective reality, revealed in *L'Endormie*, was his feeling of the incompatibility of yearning and gratification. At the moment of sudden belief there came, along with joy, a direct menace to the private sanctuary where the tortured youth could retreat to take a somber pride in his solitary martyrdom.

His need of God's love proved the stronger, however, and his objections to formal conversion gradually gave ground during the years that followed his illumination: ". . . each day my objections grew weaker . . ." (p. 195). When he finally capitulated, on December 25, 1890, he felt that he had survived the greatest crisis of his life and, like his idol in *Une Saison en Enfer*, that he too had experienced "that agony of thought about which Rimbaud had written: 'The spiritual fight is as brutal as physical combat. A hard night! the dried blood smokes on my face!' " (*"Ma Conversion,"* p. 192).

If the victory Claudel had just won over his pride provided a great spiritual uplift, it did not transform him, change his temperament, or tame and convert the inner man.[11] His love-quest had not been christianized, nor had he yet convinced himself, as he would later, that love without gratification here on earth was a higher order of bliss than human love.[12] He had yet to train himself to *feel*, not merely to believe, that love is magnified when it transcends the sensory world to become an exclusively spiritual entity.

Claudel's poetic vocation received its main impetus during the period immediately following his illumination at Notre-Dame in 1886. The passion and the diffuse creative energy that fed his self-centered dream of love had indeed become channelled and focused, following his religious experience, but toward poetic activity, with the Muse of Poetry replacing the nymph of *L'Endormie*. From Notre-Dame Claudel emerged a serious poet: "Curiously enough, the awakening of my soul" he writes, "and that of my poetic faculties was taking place simultaneously" (*"Ma Conversion,"* p. 194). The ever alert poet in him was quick to derive from his spiritual experience the nucleus of a poetic program, as he frankly explained to Jean Amrouche, in *Mémoires improvisés*:[13] "The task of according [*d'arranger ensemble*] the two worlds, of making this world coincide with the other, has been the preoccupation of my whole life, and it was when I walked out of Notre-Dame that I understood the immensity of this enterprise" (p. 51).

Almost on the threshold of Notre-Dame, so to speak, Claudel

asked himself to what specific use, within the framework of his newfound faith, he would put his poetic gift. That this question should have at once solicited his attention reveals the exigencies of his creative temperament and, specifically, his need for the irresistible pleasure he derived from poetic activity.[14] "A trait of his nature," notes Henri Guillemin, "is his devouring passion for poetry. And I mean here his ability, discovered early and savored without restraint, to respond with exceptional intensity to the ecstatic pleasures of artistic activity" (RP, May 1955, p. 94).

This consuming passion for the Muses (no less than that for Galaxaure) is, however, in direct conflict with the call to total renunciation which, at least in theory, he knew could follow his sudden "conversion" of 1886. "No convert has been spared the anguish," he writes to Louis Massignon in 1908, "of wondering whether God, who asked him to take a first step, will not ask him to take a second" (Chaigne, Vie, p. 84). This second step, which leads to sainthood, did not concern Claudel at once, nor is there any evidence that during the four years between his illumination and his formal conversion (1886-1890) he considered it at all. He was far too involved in the problems which his identification with Rimbaud had brought to the surface. "For four years Rimbaud's thought was in ferment in me" he wrote in L'Oeil écoute. This "fermentation," which has never been studied fully, this "presence" of Rimbaud in Claudel lasted in fact throughout his life. Henri Guillemin cites the aging poet as having said, "I remember being a poet at the age of seven" (RP, May 1955, p. 94). Does this merely reflect conceit and the need to appear a prodigy?[15] Guillemin invites us to think so and begs the reader's indulgence for his friend ("Let us not quibble about the age" RP, May 1955, p. 94). But obviously we must, for Claudel was here unconsciously using a reminiscence of Rimbaud's "Les Poètes de sept ans."

If we try to understand the nature of Claudel's identification with Rimbaud, still active more than half a century after the original encounter, the word that comes to mind to characterize it is incarnation. When Claudel, oppressed and sick with despair, stumbled upon the poetry of Rimbaud—in whom, as we have indicated, he found a spiritual brother—he "became" Rimbaud and clung to him to escape from himself. But in the presence of Rimbaud he grew acutely conscious of conflicting tendencies in his own nature, tendencies which he shared with Rimbaud. In the "mystic in a savage state" whom Claudel saw in Rimbaud— this characterizes Claudel too, through his identification with Rimbaud—the "savage" was too wild and would have to be tamed to protect the "mystic." Hence the need for a dramatic confrontation.

It took place in *Tête d'Or* (1889), Claudel's first major play, and was continued in *La Ville* (1890). These plays of revolt, which give free rein to violence, murder and anarchy, in effect helped Claudel detach himself from Rimbaud (though he never admitted this, if indeed he understood it) as he sought the antidote he needed to his own despair, and on December 25, 1890, he was formally converted to Catholicism.

NOTES

[1] *L'Endormie*, in Paul Claudel, *Théâtre*, Bibliothèque de la Pléiade (Paris: Gallimard, 1956), I, 3-18. See *Bulletin de la Société Paul Claudel*, No. 5, December 1960, pp. 11-12; No. 6, Feb. 1961, pp. 14-15, for the most authoritative discussion of the composition date of *L'Endormie*.

[2] See Robert Mallet's introduction to *André Suarès et Paul Claudel: Correspondance*, p. 13.

[3] *RP*, April 1955, p. 28.

[4] Yves Bonnefoy, *Rimbaud par lui-même* (Paris: Editions du Seuil, 1961), pp. 14-15.

[5] ". . . it was in May, 1886, at the Luxembourg. I had just purchased a copy of *La Vogue* which contained the first installment of *Illuminations* [specifically, the first sixteen poems from "*Après le Déluge*" to "*Ornières*". I cannot call it anything else but a veritable illumination. My life was completely transformed by these few fragments . . ." Paul Claudel, *Mémoires improvisés* (Paris: Gallimard, 1954), p. 27.

[6] Before leaving *L'Endormie*, it should be noted that Jean-Paul Weber, commenting on the symbolic meaning of Claudel's Galaxaure (the name occurs in Hesiod's *Theogony* (353) in a list of Nereids, and in Homer's "Hymn to Ceres" (424), has proposed an interpretation based on a pun: he would have "gala/xaure" stand for "lait/sûr" or sour milk [Jean-Paul Weber, "Paul Claudel," *Genèse de l'oeuvre poétique* (Paris: Gallimard, 1960), pp. 338-387. The name Galaxaure actually derives from Greek roots meaning milk and wind.] This stems from his analysis of the frequency of breast symbolism in Claudel's work. Weber's thesis is that a traumatic breast weaning experi-

ence (for which, however, he offers no evidence) is at the root of the poet's creative impulse. It would indeed be easy to bring forward other etymological puns, supporting elaborate interpretations with equal gratuity. For example: "xaure-xêros" (dry). Did not Claudel's sea-nymph emerge from the waters to dry her body on earth, and was she not subsequently turned into a sleeping beauty by the magic of an earthly flower? Is not her sin, therefore, to have wanted to taste the fruit of the earth, leaving the realm of the primordial waters in order to become an earth-bound, mortal woman? The first flower she tastes casts a spell on her which only her love for a human being can break, and only a poet's words can make her visualize, in her sleep, the lover whose image she will so yearn to clasp that her desire will break the spell. This interpretation is perfectly plausible except, of course, that its etymological premise, as in Weber, is gratuitous. Why not also point out that the Fall and the Redemption of Man through the love of Christ is already implicit in this pre-conversion play? After all, is not Danse-la-Nuit, representing the pagan world, a diabolical figure, the Mystifier who delights in preventing Man's salvation through love? Would it not follow that the young Claudel, even before his conversion, was experiencing life in Catholic terms and yearning for a Catholic solution to his despair? These assumptions are supported by the multiple resonances of this embryonic text. For in *L'Endormie*, as Eugène Roberto has rightly put it, "nothing is resolved . . . everything is in question." (Eugène Roberto, "L'Endormie," *Cahiers Paul Claudel* (Paris: Gallimard, 1960) , II, 89-94.)

7 "Ma Conversion" was reprinted in *Contacts et Circonstances* (1940) and in Volume XVI of the *Oeuvres Complètes*.

8 Cf. ". . . yes, Jesus was the Son of God. He had singled me out, me Paul, from among all men and was promising me His love" (*OC*, XVI, 193) .

9 Some twenty years later, in a letter to Jacques Rivière, he drew a monstrous picture of this naturalistic world view he had fought so hard to preserve: "this hideous world of Taine, of Renan and the other Molochs of the 19th century . . . this prison . . . this mechanistic monster, governed exclusively by rigid laws believed, most outrageously, to be knowable and even teachable!" [Jacques Rivière et Paul Claudel: *Correspondance: 1907-1914* (Paris: Plon 1926), pp. 142-143.]

10 See Chaigne, *Vie*, p. 13; also Henri Guillemin, *RP*, April 1955, pp. 29-30.

11 Cf. Claudel to Jacques Rivière: "You must gradually learn to tame your sub-conscious" (Corresp. Cl./Riv., p. 91) .

12 Many years later Claudel writes bluntly to Rivière, who feared that Catholicism might limit, "shrink" he thought, his capacity and freedom to love: "Human love is beautiful only when not gratified . . . as for the pleasures of love fulfilled, no writer has ever described them, for they do not exist. The paradise which would consist in possession of a woman's body and soul as an end in itself seems to me undistinguish-able from hell" (*Corresp.* pp. 260; 262) .

13 Paul Claudel, *Mémoires improvisés* (Paris: Gallimard, 1954) . This is the tran-scribed record of forty-two radio interviews conducted by Jean Amrouche, taped in 1950 and broadcast on the French National Radio (Chaîne Nationale) from May 21 to July 12, 1951, and from October 1, 1951 to February 14, 1952.

14 Cf. the opening lines of *"La Muse qui est la Grâce,"* *Oeuvre poétique*, Bibliothèque de la Pléiade (Paris: Gallimard, 1957) , p. 263. Claudel equates poetic activity with drunkenness.

15 Claudel admitted to Guillemin that the long accepted composition date of *L'Endormie* (1882-3) was a fabrication, to make it appear that he was 14, not 18 years old when he wrote it!

CHAPTER II

The Confrontation with Rimbaud

Claudel has stated often that he drank at Rimbaud's spring, and we would be ill-inspired indeed if we did not take him at his word. Viewed as a phase in Claudel's spiritual evolution, *Tête d'Or* and *La Ville* stand as monuments to the rôle Rimbaud played in his new orientation. They are the very stage on which their author confronted Rimbaud, on which he transposed and re-enacted his own *"saison en enfer."* These two plays, composed in 1889 and 1890 respectively,[1] reveal important aspects of his inner struggle, in his quest for a *modus vivendi* between 1886 and 1890. These aspects can be said to reflect, roughly, the progress of his absorption of the works of Rimbaud, whom he had been idolizing for the last three years.

It should be understood that we are not confronted here with the familiar problem of a literary influence, born of temperamental affinities. There seems to have been in Claudel a proudly repressed need to escape from self, to protect himself from self through some form of worship, and this need, suddenly made acute by the discovery of Rimbaud, a kindred spirit who was also a great poet, transformed Rimbaud into an object of worship. This quasi-incarnation must soon have proved unsatisfactory, Claudel's life-long public allegiance to Rimbaud notwithstanding. If, in the first year or two of this extra-literary relationship, Claudel was boundlessly grateful to Rimbaud for having reached out, with his poetry, to the core of his loneliness, by the time he was writing *Tête d'Or* he must have realized that, in radical contrast with Rimbaud, his own solidly anchored bourgeois values and early religious training[2] demanded a harbor in which to moor his *"bateau ivre,"* which his diplomatic career and his formal conversion to Catholicism would soon provide.

As Jean Amrouche has pointed out, Claudel wished to distinguish himself from Rimbaud in one major respect: unlike the author of *Season in Hell,* sublime but defeated, he would be a victor and distinguish himself from his spiritual brother by his victory (*Cahiers,* I, 131). He yearned to give a positive value to the "negative flame," the "burning and ferocious void" which Jacques Rivière saw in Rimbaud and which the author of *Tête d'Or* recognized in himself. In sum, having escaped from self through worship of Rimbaud, he soon sought to protect himself from Rimbaud's excesses, which echoed dangerously in himself.

Here too, incidentally, even in relation to his beloved Rimbaud, a certain polarity, so fundamental to his mode of feeling, is evident in Claudel: the same opposing forces which cause him to resist with all his might, while powerfully lured by them, the neopagan elements of his nature. Unlike Rimbaud, he fears these powerful drives while unwilling to check them, fears that they might get out of control; and control, solemnly pledged and dutifully cultivated, is for him the key that liberates man from self, that opens the door to felicity.[3] This is hardly a duplicate of Rimbaud's "key" to felicity, whether the "old" one that gave access to the illusory, neopagan *"festin ancien,"* or the "new" one which, in *Saison en Enfer,* a chastened Rimbaud identifies with charity.[4]

In the human equation, love neutralizes fear, and the measure of Claudel's hunger for love is the measure of his fear of tendencies in himself which he considered destructive. Drawn as Claudel was to Rimbaud, he recognized such tendencies in him as, for instance, Rimbaud's almost hysterical anger at the surrounding world. If we consider the naturalistic determinism of the day, which Claudel hated as Rimbaud hated his own stifling world, the two portraits seem to blend together: *"Je meurs de soif, j'étouffe, je ne puis crier* [I am dying of thirst, I am choking,

I cannot cry out]"[5] could have been written by Cébès/Claudel as well as by Rimbaud.

Claudel must have felt that Rimbaud's revolt went too far, that it was an all-out rebellion against the humiliation and inescapability of existence itself, or, in Jacques Rivière's words, against the human condition, against the physical and astronomical conditions of the universe. Nothing could be less attractive to Claudel, and in this respect he and Rimbaud stand at opposite poles. The very phrase Rivière uses here, in fact, characterizes the cause Claudel will soon espouse, that of "Gatherer of the Earth," of minstrel of the cosmic world and spokesman for the Creation.

During these years of struggle (1886-1890), Claudel's mystical experience stands faithfully in the background, a constant reminder that Rimbaud erred sadly, and recognized it, judging from *Saison en Enfer*, when he enlisted voyancy and flirted with insanity in his pursuit of felicity. In *Tête d'Or* Claudel attempts to tame and re-channel the Rimbaud in himself. This he does by giving Simon Agnel, his self-centered hero and would-be world conqueror, free rein, and allowing him to destroy himself, a device which recurs in later works (see especially *L'Echange* and *Partage*). As he composes this play (1889), he is nearing the end of his four years of struggle against the summons to conversion. The following year he formally "surrenders" to Catholicism.

The first version of the play, written in 1889, actually continues Act IV of *Une Mort prématurée*, originally a four-act play, composed in 1888, which Claudel destroyed except for the last act, later published as *Fragment d'un drame*.[6] This act contains two scenes and three characters. In the first scene, a fourteen-line monologue, a brother (identified simply as "The Brother") takes solemn leave of his sister (Marie) against a gloomy background of quarrels, grudges and crimes which cannot be reliably reconstructed. The brother's radical despair is evident in his apparent intention to commit suicide and in his bitter description of man and society, reminiscent of Claudel's pre-conversion mood:

> *Les vieux sorciers nus à quatre pattes comme des*
> *Loups*
> *Jappent contre le mur des cimetières;*
> *Des querelles lugubres divisent les Fils de la Fosse;*
> *Et sur sa colline Satan,*
> *La détestable brute à trompe de sanglier, siège et*
> *grogne!*
> *Allons!*
> *J'ai fait ce qu'il m'a plu de faire, et je mourrai*
> *par moi.*
>
> (Th. I, 21)

[The naked old sorcerers, on all fours like Wolves
Yelp at the cemetery walls;
Sullen quarrels divide the Sons of the Grave;
And enthroned on his hill, Satan,
That loathsome swine-faced beast, is grunting!
Enough!
I have done what I wanted, and I will die by my own
    hand.]

In the second scene Marie's lover, Henri, visits her for the last time. His secret desire is to extricate himself from a relationship which, as Marie bitterly explains, reaches fulfillment only in death:

> *Mais il y a une chose meilleure que tout: c'est*
> *de dormir*
> *Dans le sommeil du sang et de la mort! puisse ceci*
> *Nous arriver bientôt à tous deux, comme conclusion*
> *à notre scène tragique!* (p. 25)

[But there is one thing better than all others:
    to sink

Into the sleep of blood and death! May this
Soon happen to both of us, to conclude our tragic
  scene!]

Had Marie addressed herself to the Mesa of the third act of
Partage de Midi, she would have been understood. But the time
is 1888, not 1905, and she is facing the future Tête d'Or, who
tells her:

> . . . *si je dois mourir, non lentement*
> *Mais égorgé et tout d'un coup, c'est bien.*
> *Je répandrai cette libation. Du moins*
> *Serai-je d'une très belle veuve pleuré.* (p. 24)

> [. . . if I must die, it should not be slowly—
> Better that my throat were suddenly slit.
> I will pour out this libation. At least
> I will be wept over by a most beautiful widow.]

In *Tête d'Or,* the brother of *Une Mort prématurée* becomes
Cébès, Henri reappears as Simon Agnel and Marie is none other
than Simon's dead mistress whom Simon is burying as the play
opens. The general despair of Cébès expressed in Part I of the
play ceases the moment his blind worship of Simon Agnel begins,
sealed and consecrated by a ritualistic blood ceremony. Cébès
worships at Simon's feet without question, out of a need to worship a law, an order outside himself which he begs his elder to
provide. For like Claudel, Cébès knows how it feels to be totally
bereft of happiness, *"la privation de tout bonheur"* (p. 41).

Claudel's incarnation of Rimbaud is acted out by young Cébès
who surrenders his will to Simon Agnel, the future Tête d'Or.
There can be little doubt that Cébès is a self-portrait fashioned
out of the poet's most tortured pre-Rimbaud moods and
thoughts.[7] These, and the world in which he lives, or rather
Cébès/Claudel's horrible image of it, reflecting his view of naturalism, hold out no hope whatever of happiness:[8]

Cébès: . . . *Il y a des gens dont les yeux*
Fondent comme des nèfles fendues qui laissent couler
  leurs pépins.
Et des jeunes filles qui, des années,
Hurlent sur le dos, et dont le maigre tas d'ossements
  comme des sarments se recroquevillent,
Chuintent une liqueur cadavérique.
Et des nouveau-nés monstrueux, des hommes ayant un
  mufle de veau,
Et des enfants violés et tués par leurs pères,
Et des vieillards qui sentent leur vie pourrir et,
  vivants, se revêtent de leur fosse dégoûtante!
Toutes les maladies veillent sur nous, l'ulcère et
  l'abcès, le cancer qui ronge la langue et la lippe;
  un malade lève son masque couvert de larves infectes!
La phtisie fait son feu; les parties honteuses moisissent
  comme le bois; et le sac du ventre
Crève et vide dehors les entrailles et les excréments.
N'est-ce pas horrible! mais notre vie
Qui se fait de fête à un repas de larves s'empiffre
Jusqu'à ce que, comme un chien qui vomit des morceaux
  de viande,
Le ventre bourré se révolte et qu'on rende gorge sur
  la table. (Th. I, 41)

[*Cébès:* . . . There are people whose eyes
Crumble like burst medlars spilling their seeds.
And young girls who, year after year,
Howl on their backs, and whose paltry skeletons
  shrivel like vine shoots,
And hiss out a cadaverous liqueur.
And monstrous new-born babies, bull-faced men,
Children raped and slaughtered by their fathers
And old men who smell the putrefaction of their
  lives and, still living, put on the apparel
  of their disgusting graves!
All the diseases dog our tracks: the ulcer and

the abscess, the cancer which gnaws away
    tongue and lip; a sick man lifts his mask,
    crawling with infected worms!
Consumption spreads its fire; the organs of shame
    rot like wood; and the belly's sac
Bursts and pours out entrails and excrement.
Horrible! But our life,
Which feasts on a repast of grubs, gorges itself,
Until, like a dog which spews up scraps of meat,
The crammed belly revolts, and vomits onto the table.]

How much of Claudel's own despair went into Cébès, how closely he meant to identify with his character is evident from Cébès's opening monologue in the play and from some of Claudel's own early verse, in *Premiers Vers*, where he is obviously talking about himself:

Cébès: *Me voici,*
Imbécile, ignorant,
Homme nouveau devant les choses inconnues,
Et je tourne la face vers l'Année et l'arche
    pluvieuse, j'ai plein mon coeur d'ennui!
Je ne sais rien et je ne peux rien. Que dire?
    Que faire? A quoi emploierai-je ces mains
    qui pendent? ces pieds qui m'emmènent comme
    les songes? (*Tête d'Or, Th.* I, 31)

[*Cébès:* Here I am,
An ignorant imbecile,
A new man confronting unknown things,
And I turn my face toward the Year and the rainy
    skies and boredom fills my heart!
I know nothing and can do nothing. What can I
    say? What can I do? How can I use these
    dangling hands, these feet which lead me
    on as does a dream?]

Mes yeux sont pleins de nuit et mon coeur est
  plein d'eau!
. . . Et si je marche, où que j'arrive! il n'y
  a rien,
Et le pied conduit l'autre pied d'où il vient.
                          (Premiers Vers, OP, p. 9)

[Night fills my eyes, and water my heart!
I walk but wherever I arrive there is nothing,
And one foot pulls the other after it.]

The rather chaotic first version of the play leaves unclear the nature of Simon's inner struggle in Part I.[9] In the second version of 1894, this scene is eliminated and replaced by a scene of communion with the earth at the foot of a richly symbolic tree: "I wish to question you, deep-reaching roots, and that primordial depth of the earth whence you draw your strength" (p. 183). Here Simon's secret yearning for total self-reliance is revealed, at the moment he accepts the worship of Cébès (p. 186).

Here, as in the later *Partage,* the object of love, be it Simon Agnel in *Tête d'Or* or Rimbaud in Claudel's life, is a false idol. Cébès, in quest of a new formula for living, discovers this as he understands that he must die in order to be reborn. His death foreshadows the death of his godhead, Tête d'Or. Simon's determined plan to dominate and transcend the universe, like Rimbaud's, is destined to leave him empty-handed, crushed in the lonely vanity of total self-reliance. At the end of his journey, Tête d'Or points to a solution by accepting the ministrations of the Princess, who is solemnly invested with the attributes of her symbolic role as savior. The old Emperor her father, symbol of a meaningless and decaying world, is dead. The usurper dies too, his eyes opened too late onto the vaingloriousness of human ambitions.[10] As he dies, he orders that the Princess be crowned Queen. She, in turn, as a Princess/Christ symbol, must die, that man, cleansed and purified, may live in the image of God.

If our assumption that *Tête d'Or* dramatizes Claudel's temporary incarnation of Rimbaud is correct, Cébès would represent the pre-Rimbaud Claudel; the link with Rimbaud is symbolically expressed in the play by the pact of blood between Cébès and Simon; the Rimbaud-Claudel incarnation is then explored. Cébès dies with the old civilization with which he is identified. Tête d'Or, at the peak of his glory, discovers before dying the vanity of worldly ambitions and, by ordering the coronation of the Princess/Christ, paves the way for the triumph of the Christian Church.

One year after *Tête d'Or,* Claudel wrote the first version of *La Ville.* This version, which has recently been described as "a rough draft of no interest,"[11] yields important insights into the nature of Claudel's continuing dialogue with Rimbaud. There emerges from it the first outline of Claudel's future poetics, born of his efforts to explore and formulate, in this year which will witness his formal conversion (December 25, 1890), a poetic program. Madaule acknowledges the importance of the first version, but only in passing, while discussing the 1897 version, and then merely to stress that the play reflects Claudel's formal return to Catholicism (p. 25).[12]

To be sure, in comparison with the second, this first version is chaotic, the delineation of characters irritatingly vague. Nevertheless, if we disregard the first version of this play, inferior as it is to the later one, we overlook an important phase in the evolution of the poet's thought. Claudel has so often repeated that he was all his characters, that we ought to try taking him at his word—in the sense that his plays, read in the order of their composition, reflect his continuous dialogue with self, the dramatic discourse of his inner voices.

What appears to have taken place in *La Ville* is a fragmentation of the characters of *Tête d'Or,* as a result of Claudel's need to explore further, and on a broader canvas, certain facets of himself involving poetic activity, not touched upon in the first play. Indeed, *La Ville* suffers from over-fragmentation. There

are some twenty male characters and a host of female "voices."
Of these, Ly and Coeuvre, both poets, are of particular interest
here.

It would appear that Ly is a new Cébès, revived to restate and
debate further that unhappy youth's obsessive question: "*Tous
les hommes posent un désir devant eux,/A savoir, que sais-je?*
[All men desire the answer to one question/Namely, what do I
know]" (p. 311). One is reminded at once of Cébès's, "Here I
am, an ignorant imbecile . . ." (*Tête d'Or*, p. 31). Ly's link to
Claudel/Cébès is unmistakable. He is a poet—the first "pro-
fessional" poet in Claudel's works, if we disregard the grotesque
youth of *L'Endormie*. With simple naïveté he seeks an answer
to the world's riddles ("Tell me," he asks Besme, "what do you
think about the world? perhaps I don't see clearly" p. 311). The
answer he gets is a message of doom, since materialism rules and
the gods are dead (". . . there are no more gods"). His only
recourse, he is told, is to let his poet's imagination beautify the
world ("Go and transform your misery" p. 312). As for Besme,
he is the new man-made god (". . . and thus I was made a god"
p. 313)—an unhappy god at that ("Would that I had never been
born" p. 313), who despises the very humanity over which he
reigns ("As I pass by them, I feel like spitting on those scoun-
drels" p. 313). His only consolation is to listen to the poet, like
Saul to David's harp:

> *O toi qui comme la langue résides dans un lieu obscur!*
> *Tu sais peu de choses et je ne t'appellerai point sage;*
>   *et cependant quand tu parles j'écoute.*
> *Quand tu parles ainsi qu'un homme qui se souvient,*
> *J'écoute; et c'est comme une branche quand un oiseau*
>   *pose dessus* [sic].
> *O toi qui seul d'entre tous les hommes fais entendre*
>   *un langage paisible!* (p. 311)

[O you who, like the word, inhabit a dark place!
You know little, and I would not call you wise; never-

theless, I listen when you speak.
When you speak as one who remembers
I listen; and it is like a branch when a bird settles
    on it.
Oh you who alone among men give utterance to a peace-
    ful language!]

Ly's image of himself is that of the ancient poets chosen as
mere instruments by the Muses, endowed with a mysterious gift
of inspiration over which there is no control and which passes
comprehension:

Ecoute, ô Besme!
Je ne parle pas selon ce que je veux, d'abord le
    souffle m'est enlevé!
Et de nouveau, de l'existence de la vie se soulève
    le désir de respirer!
Et j'absorbe l'air, et le coeur profond, baigné,
Il dit, et je restitue une parole;
Et alors je sais ce que j'ai dit. Et telle est ma joie.
    (p. 311)

[Listen, O Besme!
I do not will what I speak; first, breath is withdrawn
    from me!
And anew, there arises from the existence of life
    itself the desire to breathe,
And I absorb the air, and the profound heart, bathed,
Speaks, and I restore a word;
And then I know what I have said. And such is my
    joy.]

This is the initial formulation of Claudel's concept of poetic
inspiration.[13] Conceived a few months before his formal conversion, it may have facilitated that conversion, for this neopagan
concept of the "elect" poet provides a justification for the poetic
vocation, when transposed to the Christian system.

As for Coeuvre, he helps us to see that the first two acts of the play contain a further commentary on the Claudel-Rimbaud drama. When Coeuvre's arrival is announced, Ly rises to flee ("Let us leave before he comes, for I love him not!" p. 321). Ly's explanation of this reflex to flee may well contain Claudel's only confession—and that a veiled one—of his secret envy of Rimbaud's genius—to be sure, overshadowed by and by no means incompatible with worship:

Heureux
Celui à qui la Muse a lissé les cheveux avec la
*   paume de ses mains,*
Celui à qui elle a mis un peu de miel au-dessous
*   de la langue! il ne se souciera plus des*
*   maux!*
Et moi, si je l'entends,
Je ne me soucie plus de moi, mais je joins les
*   mains,*
Et je place en lui ma surprise, et, le regardant,
*   je pleure de joie et de jalousie.*
Que le chef de guerre secoue sa crosse quand, non
*   né, il entend le long cri de la trompette!*
Mes larmes coulent quand j'entends le son heureux
*   de la lyre.* (p. 321)

[Happy is he
Whose hair the Muse has smoothed with the palm
    of her hand,
Under whose tongue she has put honey! He will
    no longer be beset by care!
And I, if I hear him,
No longer care about myself, but join my hands,
And entrust to him my surprise; and, looking at
    him, I weep with joy and jealousy.
Let the yet unborn warrior brandish his sword when
    he hears the long wail of the trumpet!
My tears flow when I hear the happy sound of the
    lyre.]

Ly is fascinated by Coeuvre and remains to engage him in a conversation which contains strangely haunting echoes of Rimbaud:

> *Ly: Coeuvre! j'avais mis des espérances en toi.*
>
> . . . .
>
> *Mais toi, tout à coup, nous t'avons vu obscurcir
> le soleil . . .*
>
> . . . .
>
> *Ne médite pas de te taire et de retirer tes mains
> du milieu de nous, ô toi qui te tiens ici
> avec un pouvoir de changement!* (p. 324)

> [*Ly*: Coeuvre! I have put my hopes in you.
>
> . . . .
>
> But suddenly we have seen you darken the sun . . .
>
> . . . .
>
> Do not contemplate falling silent and withdrawing
> your hands from among us, O you who stand
> here with a power for change!]

Claudel would seem here to be weighing Rimbaud's withdrawal and his own desire to preserve Rimbaud as an ideal. Coeuvre's reply reveals the direction which Claudel's thought is beginning to take, namely that poetic activity pursued as an end in itself may well be useless self-indulgence and even self-deception:

> . . . *que suis-je? quel homme mettant sa main à ma bouche
> aura de moi une parole qui serve? . . . jadis, faisant sortir
> une vision de mon coeur . . . je me la racontais à moi-même,
> . . . Mais à présent . . . je suis troublé! . . . Car ma crainte
> est de mentir.* (pp. 324-325)[14]

> [. . . What am I? What man, putting his hand to my
> mouth, would take from me a word that would be of use?
> . . . formerly, drawing out a vision from my heart . . . I
> would recount it to myself, . . . But now . . . I am troubled!
> . . . For I fear to lie.]

In this dialogue between Ly and Coeuvre we can sense Claudel's efforts to formulate his poetics. His vocation of poet-priest, of "Father of the Arts" (see "*La Catastrophe d'Igitur*," *OC*, XV, 117), has not yet clearly emerged. This explains why in *La Ville* the poet's rôle is split between Ly and Coeuvre, and why a *stranger* (not Coeuvre himself, as in the second version of the play) is the bearer of the Christian message in the last act.

When in the third act Avare leaves his victorious friends, never to return, Claudel symbolically dissociates himself from Tête d'Or and from that part of Rimbaud which contributed to the making of Tête d'Or. The similarity of attitudes in Avare and Rimbaud is underscored by Jacques Madaule, who wonders: "Will Avare reconstruct what he has destroyed?" (*Drame*, p. 22), and answers: "No, but he goes away having finished his task. . . . He leaves, as Rimbaud left . . ." (p. 23). In the second version of the play, it is Coeuvre who comes back with the new message. In this we see that the Coeuvre of the earlier version (1890), so reminiscent of both Rimbaud *and* the future Claudel, was indeed a transitional figure. He reappears seven years later fully "claudelized" in *La Ville* II (1897).

The third act of *La Ville*, by its climate of ideas, immediately reflects the accomplished conversion. Indeed, the third act debates it, attempts to justify it, and, thanks to an understandable *parti-pris*, succeeds in converting to Catholicism the Jacobin leaders of the successful revolution.

To their own surprise, these colorful revolutionary leaders discover the meaninglessness of their victory. They resist as best they can the onslaughts of the most consummate proselytism, but lack the eloquence and the argumentation of a Rivière, a Suarès, or a Gide:

Ivors: *Non. Je ne me résous point à te croire.*
Le Troisième Consacré: *Sois prudent en ce cas! Va-t'en!*
　Peut-être même
Déjà qu'il est d'un peu de temps trop tard.

Ne fais pas une demande pour rire. N'appelle pas
Le Lion qui ne te voit pas, par moquerie.
De peur que, s'approchant de toi, que répondras-tu, s'il
  dit: J'ai faim? (p. 402)
[*Ivors*: No. I cannot consent to believe you.
The Third Initiate: In that case be careful!
  Leave! Perhaps
It is already a little too late.
Do not make a request in jest. Do not mock-
  ingly call
The Lion who does not see you
For fear that, coming to you, he would say:
  I am hungry, and what would you reply?]

Bewildered, their only recourse is to turn for advice to their hesitant but tempted leader who surrenders:

Palfer: *Ivors, nous attendons que tu parles.*
Ivors: *Tu le veux? Et moi, je me sens porté*
  aussi à faire une promesse à l'Etre . . .
    Th. I, 406)
[*Palfer*: Ivors, we are waiting for you to speak.
Ivors: You wish me to? For myself, I also feel
  moved to make a promise to the Supreme Being . . .]

The entire last act of *La Ville* is Claudel's first, most eloquent and most successful proselytizing effort. The vigor of his proselytism, sprung full-grown from his new faith, is worth pondering. Tête d'Or's conquering impulse would seem to have survived here, but the weapons have changed. We are now facing a Christian crusader whose zeal has temporarily overcome his own resistance to conversion, generated mainly by his consuming passion for poetic activity.

The solemn and fervent tone of Act Three of *La Ville* should not mislead us. Claudel will, of course, observe his formal pact with the Church, but he is far from the equilibrium and the serenity he seeks. Three years later he writes: ". . . life is such a serious and solemn undertaking, we must account with utmost precision for each half minute of it . . . and especially those of us who cannot avail themselves of the excuse that the truth was not revealed to them. There is something that I must say and I cannot and will not relent until I succeed in saying it. God, who has placed it in me so that I may reveal it through toil and suffering, knows that my feeble words give me no joy, except the pleasure of producing them; it is to answer this injunction that I have sold my freedom and renounced all interests in life" (Letter of 1893 to Maurice Pottecher, in *Cahiers* I, 80-81).

Claudel is already clerking in God's service, patiently searching his soul for the sacred message he must express, understand and accept. In 1892 he will compose the first version of *La Jeune Fille Violaine*,[15] which reveals for the first time his concern with total renunciation. It is this version of *Violaine* that we must give particular attention to if we wish to explore the genesis of the renunciation theme in Claudel.[16]

NOTES

[1] *Tête d'Or, Th.* I, 31-167, was first published anonymously by the Librairie de l'Art Indépendant in 1890. *La Ville, Th.* I, 305-413, was first published, also anonymously, by the same publisher in 1893.

[2] See H. Guillemin, " 'La Conversion' de Paul Claudel" in *EC*, 1957, Vol. 25.

[3] Cf. "*Prière pour le dimanche matin*," written twenty years later:

Gardons ce serment entre nous! scellez-moi de peur
  que je ne me dissipe.
Humanité de Dieu sur ma langue, consignez mon coeur
  et mon principe. (*Corona benignitatis anni
  Dei, OP,* 371)

[Keep this oath of ours! Enfold me for fear that
  I dissipate myself.
Humanity of God on my tongue, enclose my heart and
  my principle.]

[4] Arthur Rimbaud, *Une Saison en Enfer, Oeuvres complètes,* Bibliothèque de la Pléiade (Paris: Gallimard, 1954), p. 219.

[5] Rimbaud, *OC,* p. 226.

[6] *Fragment d'un drame* was first published in the May, 1892, issue of *La Revue indépendante* under the title, *Morceau d'un drame.* It was reprinted in 1931 as *Fragment d'un drame* in *Bibliographie des oeuvres de Paul Claudel: de Tête d'Or (1890)*

au Soulier de Satin (1929), précédée de "Fragment d'un drame" (1891), by Benoist-Méchin and Auguste Blaizot (Paris: Blaizot, 1931), pp. 7-18. According to Guillemin (*RP*, May 1955, p. 92, n.3), Claudel destroyed the original play, *Une Mort prématurée*, "because of his family." Guillemin reports that he was never able to get Claudel to tell him the content of the destroyed play.

7 See the recently published letter of Claudel to Albert Mockel, written in 1890, the only known letter on the subject of *Tête d'Or* contemporary with the work itself. "The idea of this book is as follows: in the absence of happiness, desire alone subsists. A tragic situation! I have an immense need of happiness and find nothing in the visible world to satisfy it. Is this due to denial or lack? [*Est-ce refus ou manque?*] This is a mystery which requires to be explored with torch and sword" (*Cahiers*, I, 140). "*Est-ce refus ou manque?*" is rather ambiguous, but probably means, "have I been excluded" (i.e. refused access to happiness) and "have I so far failed through lack of effort or determination?" In different terms, Rimbaud raises essentially the same question about himself: he feels doomed in advance as a member of an inferior or "*gaulois*" race, and wonders whether he can, through voyancy and the creation of a new language, reach, and maintain himself in, a state of bliss.

8 See the chapter on Claudel in Henri Guillemin's *Zola, légende ou vérité* (Paris: Juillard, 1960).

9 Henri Guillemin suggests rather convincingly (*EC*, Vol. 25, p. 30) that Simon is here convulsively rejecting a summons to conversion, thus enacting Claudel's own resistance to submission.

10 Cf. Rimbaud's "*L'Impossible*" in *Saison en Enfer, OC* pp. 239-241.

11 Jean-Paul Weber, "Paul Claudel," *Genèse de l'oeuvre poétique* (Paris: Gallimard, 1960), p. 362.

12 What was not known until the publication in 1951 of the Claudel-Suarès correspondence was that the first two acts were written before the conversion, the third act afterwards. See *André Suarès et Paul Claudel: Correspondance (1904-1938)* (Paris: Gallimard, 1951), p. 36. Since all available sources give 1890 as the composition date of the entire play, with the formal conversion taking place on December 25, 1890, it would follow, though this is rather unlikely, that the last act was written in the remaining six days of 1890. The 1890 composition date suggests perhaps that Claudel had reached his decision to join the Catholic Church earlier (but when?), and had chosen to signify it on December 25 of that year.

13 It will be retained seven years later and shifted to the poet Coeuvre in the second version of the play, where Ly disappears.

14 Cf. Rimbaud's awareness of self-delusion in *Saison en Enfer*.

15 Paul Claudel, *Th.* I, 493-568.

16 The first version of *La Jeune fille Violaine* was published in 1926 by the Editions Excelsior. Claudel was never satisfied with this first version (See *MI*, 92), and evidently had no intention of publishing it. He omitted it from the 1911 edition of *Théâtre* (Paris: Mercure de France) which did, however, include both the first and second versions of *Tête d'Or* and *La Ville*.

CHAPTER III

Experiments with Renunciation

Between *La Ville* (1890) and *La Jeune fille Violaine* (1892) some important reorientation has evidently taken place. In sharp contrast with the nebulous time and place of the previous works, *Violaine* is centered on Villeneuve-sur-Fère en Tardenois, the poet's birthplace. The style of the play suggests that Claudel is making a deliberate effort to come more directly to grips with his content and with himself. His symbols are more concrete. He has abandoned his earlier "ultra-poetic and lyrical" style, as he calls it in *Mémoires improvisés* (p. 228), in favor of a vigorous realism, and is moving towards what might be called a realistic symbolism.

This change in style is not experimental nor, as Jacques Madaule suggests, merely sentimental.[1] An important shift in artistic outlook has taken place. This is confirmed by a comment Claudel makes to Pottecher the following year in a letter dated September 29, 1893: "I am . . . delighted that you are orienting yourself more and more towards realism. Truth lies in that direction" (*Cahiers* I, 82). Keeping the biography in mind, it is not inconceivable that Claudel's increasing contacts with the world of business, industry and diplomacy may have played a part in weaning him from the clannish, avant-garde world of symbolism.[2]

To the new style of *Violaine* corresponds a sharply outlined subject, the voluntary self-sacrifice of a young girl. This is Claudel's first truly Christian play, focused on the problem of evil and on the rôle of suffering in the workings of salvation. In Act I, Anne Vercors, Violaine's father, announces that he is about to undertake a voyage of indefinite duration to his native village, to look into certain unspecified matters. Before he goes, he wants to settle the matter of Violaine's marriage for purely practical reasons, so as to put Jacquin Uri, her fiancé, in charge of the farm during his absence. The truth is that he is drawn away from his daily chores, from the earth-bound slavery of his farmer existence, by the haunting memory of another land he has never seen but which he must see before he dies ("I am not from here, I remember another country! I shall go and see, . . ." *Th.* I, p. 510).[3] This is as yet unknown to his wife and daughters, and Vercors has asked Jacquin Uri to reveal it after he has gone.

When Violaine recoils at her father's suggestion that she marry without delay, Vercors hesitates and briefly loses his patriarchal composure. He understands only too well, but will choose to ignore, her own yearning for a special, uncommon destiny; for Violaine embodies the deepest aspirations of his own soul:

> . . . *et je la voyais à mon côté*
> *Toute droite, telle que la fleur appelée Impériale*
>   *et le premier-né entre les lys, belle comme*
>   *la couleur de l'or.*
> *Et j'étais plein de tristesse.* (*Th.* I, 504)

> [. . . and I saw her at my side
> Erect, like the flower called Imperial and the first-
>   sprung of the lilies, as beautiful as the color
>   of gold.
> And I was filled with sadness.]

With a sense of guilt, or, rather, because of it, Vercors decides to leave that very hour, and pointedly acknowledges that he will not be there for Violaine's wedding ("The children will have to get married without me" p. 511). His parting words to his wife seem calculated to earn him the right to leave:

Je ne t'ai point trompée avec des servantes.
Certes, je ne t'ai point trompée, mais je t'ai
*   gardé*
Ma foi. (p. 511)

[I have not deceived you with the servants.
No, I have not deceived you, but have been
    faithful to you.]

   To Violaine, who clings to him, silently sobbing, he whispers awkwardly, trying not to acknowledge her plight:

Qu'est-ce qu'il a, petite fille? Qu'est-ce qu'il
*   y a, ma petite brebis?*
Tu as échangé un mari pour ton père. (p. 513)

[What is the matter, little girl? What is it my
    little lamb?
You have exchanged a father for a husband.]

Violaine, broken-hearted, can only reply, "Alas! Father! Alas!"
(p. 513).
   One can hardly fail to realize that the father understands the implications of Violaine's marriage but wishes and hopes to avoid acknowledging them. He easily settles his account with his wife, but it is another matter to "face" Violaine, literally and figuratively (p. 512). For there is in her *"une part réservée"*—a mystical dimension which echoes in his own heart.[4]
   When he removes himself and substitutes a husband (his very words), he immolates her to his yearning to leave in order to fulfill his own destiny. Thus, already in the first act, and long before Violaine will assume the self-sacrificial rôle she is destined to play later, her immolation is being enacted in a subtle, minor key. The "little lamb" (Vercors's last endearing words) assumes the rôle of sacrificial lamb and accepts the suffering which, in Claudel's theological framework, is an essential ingredient in the workings of salvation. Before dying, in the last act, Violaine

calls Vercors's hasty departure by its right name: "My father has abandoned me" (p. 551), and Vercors himself, returning just as Violaine dies, recognizes the part he played in her martyrdom and avoids a last confrontation with her:

> Baube: *Est-ce que vous la reverrez avant qu'on*
> *lui couvre le visage?*
> Anne Vercors: *Non. L'enfant reniée*
> *S'en va furtivement.* (p. 556)

> [*Baube*: Will you see her again before they
> cover up her face?
> *Anne Vercors*: No. The disinherited child
> Leaves furtively.]

In Act II, Violaine makes her first sacrifice by allowing Jacquin Uri to think that she is no longer pure. She thereby gives her sister Bibiane, who wants to marry Uri herself, the excuse she needs to cast her from the house. What lends poignancy to this scene, and depth to the previous ones, in which Violaine rejects marriage, is the fact that, in spite of her mystical vocation, Violaine loves Jacquin with a passion unsuspected by anyone. Her complexity parallels Claudel's dual and conflicting passions for the earthly and the divine. This explains why Violaine suffers intensely when, at Bibiane's urging, her mother asks her to give up Jacquin Uri. This request, silently complied with, brings Violaine to her first crossroad on the way to total renunciation. Claudel has transposed here, in the mother's account of that scene to Bibiane, something of the sudden terror, the sensation of physical pain, and the blend of limpid joy and obscure resentment which he experienced on the day of his conversion in December, 1886 (cf. *"Ma Conversion"*):

> *Et avant qu'elle n'eût rien dit encore,*
> *Elle devint pâle comme la boue, et je vis qu'elle*
> *avait compris.*

. . . .

Elle ferma les yeux comme quelqu'un qui a reçu un
coup dans le ventre.

. . . .

Et à la fin elle rouvrit les yeux, et elle me
regardait avec une expression de douceur
et de reproche,

. . . .

Et puis elle se détourna et elle se mit à gémir. (p. 514)

[And before she said anything,
She became as pale as mud, and I saw that she had
understood.

. . . .

She shut her eyes like someone who has been struck
in the stomach.

. . . .

And at the end she opened her eyes and looked at
me with an expression of gentle reproach.

. . . .

And then she turned away and began to moan.]

At Notre-Dame, Claudel too receives a blissful-horrifying summons to assume a rare destiny—obscurely anticipated, perhaps,
but until then formless and therefore painless.

Violaine's agony, foreshadowing her martyrdom, lends both
meaning and authenticity to a vocation whose main ingredient
is suffering—freely accepted suffering. She is still rather naïvely
unaware of the extent to which this is true and considers the
sacrifice already fully consummated in Act II. This is evident
from the words she cries out after the scene of her humiliation,
as soon as her former fiancé has left: "Now, oh God! oh God!
it is all over!" (p. 521). Shortly thereafter, in the same act,
Claudel mercilessly drives Violaine towards martyrdom and
dramatizes sainthood's demands for suffering by having her
treated in an unspeakably cruel manner: Bibiane burns her sister's eyes and face with hot ashes before ordering her from the
house.

In Act III, Violaine miraculously cures Aubin, Bibiane's son, of a congenital blindness. Her swift reward is Aubin's horror at seeing Violaine's horribly burnt face ("Oh! how ugly you are! Let me go!" p. 540). This is consistent with the requirements of her martyrdom, which Claudel explores and debates in the play with relentless ingenuity. For example, in this same act Baube, unhappily married to a potential saint, defends an uncomplicated hedonistic, self-centered approach to life ("As for me, I like to laugh and be satisfied" p. 530; "And why should she [his wife, Lidine] care about others? I don't!" p. 531). Puzzled by Violaine's martyrdom, he challenges her: "How is it possible to love suffering?" (p. 532). She counters indirectly with a hedonism of her own:

> *Et je ne vis plus clair, comme quand on ferme les*
> *yeux.*
>
> . . . .
>
> *O mon Dieu! et alors je connus une autre lumière,*
> *elle est appelée lumière de la paix, avec un*
> *oeil subtil!*
> *Ainsi j'étais aveugle.*
> *Mais j'étais bien contente; et je pensais en moi-*
> *même: C'est bien fait!*
> *Oh! que j'étais tranquille!* (p. 532)

> [And everything became dark, as when one shuts
> his eyes.
>
> . . . .
>
> O my God! And then, with a penetrating eye, I
> knew another light, that called the light
> of peace!
> So, I was blind.
> But I was perfectly happy; and I thought to my-
> self: that's good!
> Oh! How serene I was!]

There are few pages which so clearly transcribe Claudel's growing preoccupation with sainthood. As Violaine explains to

Baube, sainthood is not exclusively a product of will, but a granted condition, metaphorically assimilated in the text to natural physical conditions over which there is no control:

> Baube: *N'est-il point naturel que l'homme et la femme aillent ensemble?*
> Violaine: *N'est-il point naturel que la femme nourrisse elle-même son fruit?*
> *Et pourtant souvent elle ne peut pas, parce que son lait n'est pas bon.* (p. 533)

> [*Baube*: Isn't it natural for the man and the woman to go together?
> *Violaine*: Isn't it natural for the woman to nourish her fruit herself?
> But often she cannot, because her milk is not good.]

In the final act, Violaine, her head crushed on a stone by Bibiane, is carried back to her former home; she confesses her virginity to Jacquin Uri ("I did not love this man [Baube]. There was nothing between us. I was as pure as salt, I tell you," pp. 545-546). She confides to him her sister's deeds and attempts to fulfill her saintly vocation as bearer of beatitude, by forcing Jacquin, who is bent on killing Bibiane, to open to forgiveness his violent and blood-thirsty heart:

> Jacquin Uri: *Faut que je la tue!*
> *Oh!*
> *Elle s'est collée*
> *A moi comme un serpent qui s'attache à la veine du jarret, elle s'est collée à moi comme un chancre!*
> *Je la tuerai sous mes pieds comme un betêt!*
> *Je la tuerai à coups de bêche comme un putois!* (p. 547)

[*Jacquin Uri*: I must kill her!
Oh!
She has clung
To me like a snake which fastens onto the vein in
 one's leg; she has bitten into me like a canker!
I will crush her like a beetle!
I will beat her to death with a shovel, like a
 polecat.]

She succeeds, thanks to the disarming blackmail of dying wishes
("Won't you have pity on me? Can't you see that I am dying?"
p. 547) and the eloquence of her own example:

> Violaine: *Dis-lui que je lui pardonne! dis-lui
> que je l'aime!
> Elle a très bien agi,
> A sa manière.* (p. 547)

[*Violaine*: Tell her that I forgive her! Tell her
 that I love her!
She has done the right thing,
In her own way.]

Violaine's last words represent the most dramatic moment in
her short life and the high point in the play, as they suddenly
bring humanity into focus. She has played her rôle well, hero-
ically denying herself, patiently serving as a vessel of beatitude,
as a dispenser of charity, as a humble servant in the hand of God.
But as her life draws to an end and she considers her family, she
is seized with such indescribable nausea that her speech falters,
and all she can do is to demand to be carried out of that house
at once. She will not die surrounded by the filth of a corrupted,
loveless humanity:

> Violaine: *(tâtant la main de Jacquin entre ses
> mains) La main

De cet homme que j'ai aimé. O Dieu! ô Dieu!
    j'en ai fini!
Regarde, voilà leur amour.
Mon père m'a abandonnée, ma mère, livrée; et mon
    fiancé
M'a reniée, et ma soeur . . . Emportez-moi d'ici!

. . . .

Emportez-moi d'ici, car ce n'est point ici ma maison.
J'ai cédé ma part.
Ita, pater! *Je viens! emportez-moi d'ici!*
Vers le Seigneur de la vie, vers la nourriture
    du Pain! (pp. 551-552)

[*Violaine*: (fingering Jacquin's hand)
    The hand
Of this man whom I have loved, Oh God! Oh God!
    I am done with it!
See, this is their love.
My father has abandoned me, my mother given me
    up; my fiancé
Has rejected me, and my sister . . . Take me out
    of here!

. . . .

Take me out of here, for this is no longer my
    house.
I have given up my share in it.
Ita, pater! I am coming! Take me out of here!
To the Lord of life, to the nourishment of the Bread!]

In this final outburst, Violaine passes judgment on her father, her mother, her fiancé and her sister. She thus fails, at this crucial moment of her life, to achieve sainthood. Claudel eventually realized that Violaine could not utter these bitter words and be a saint. In the second version of the play (1898), the violence of her outburst is somewhat toned down (*Th.* I, p. 634). Only in *L'Annonce faite à Marie* (1910), the third version of the same play, does Claudel fully eradicate all rancor from Violaine's

heart, making her a true saint: her leprosy requires that she
leave the house and she asks her own father to carry her out:

> Violaine: . . . *Et maintenant il faut m'emporter*
>   *d'ici.*
> Jacques Hury: *T'emporter?*
> Violaine: *Ce n'est point ici la place d'une*
>   *lépreuse pour y mourir.*
> *Faites-moi porter dans cet abri que mon père avait*
>   *construit pour les pauvres à la porte de*
>   *Monsanvierge.*
>   *(Jacques Hury fait le geste de l'emporter)*
> *Non pas vous, Jacques.*
> Jacques Hury: *Eh quoi, pas même ce dernier devoir?*
> Violaine: *C'est mon père que je veux. C'est entre*
>   *les bras de mon père que je remets mon esprit.*
>   *(Th.* II, 127-128)

> [*Violaine*: . . . And now you must take me out of
>   here.
> *Jacques Hury*: Take you out?
> *Violaine*: This is no place for a leper to die.
>   Have me carried to that shelter my father
>   built for the poor by the gates of Monsanvierge.
>   (Jacques Hury makes a move to carry her out)
> Not you, Jacques.
> *Jacques Hury*: What! Not even this last duty!
> *Violaine*: It is my father I want. I place my spirit
>   in the hands of my father.]

Claudel has attempted to explain how his first version of *Violaine* became *L'Annonce faite à Marie* (*MI,* 227). He speaks of
a gradual "settling down" of the various elements in suspension
in his mind. Imperceptibly, the subjective element was reduced,
reflecting the progressive weakening of the internal debate. It
took close to twenty years, during which the main character
evolves into a true saint and even becomes metaphorically linked

with the Holy Virgin, suggesting that by then Claudel had cut himself off from any possible identification with Violaine, had made his peace with his own yearning for sainthood. In 1892, however, Claudel is far from ready to find peace, like Violaine, in the enfolding arms of the mother Church. To establish this fact we need only read *L'Echange*,[5] written the following year in America, where Claudel began his diplomatic career.

This play is more closely related to the *Violaine* of the previous year than is generally recognized. It dramatizes Claudel's need to counterweigh his tendency towards renunciation, reflected in *Violaine*. The pendulum appears to have swung in the opposite direction.

In a letter to Mme Moreno on *L'Echange*, cited by Madaule (*Drame*, p. 34), Claudel comments on his tour of duty in America. He characterizes it as a painful slavery ("The slavery in which I found myself in America was very painful to me.") Madaule interprets this rather ambiguous statement to mean that the poet is lamenting his exile, is objecting to the tedium of consular work and is resenting "all the things which the adolescent must endure when he has become a man . . ." (*Drame*, p. 35).

No doubt all this is true, but it seems that the "slavery" in question, in view of other statements in this letter, has additional overtones and includes a veiled allusion to what Claudel felt he had given up as a requisite of conversion, namely his own freedom. He explains, for instance, that the young man of *L'Echange* who sells his wife to recover his freedom was part of a composite self-portrait, along with the other three characters: "I myself am all the characters" (*Drame*, p. 34). In addition to Louis Laine, the "young savage" with whom Claudel explicitly identifies ("I have drawn myself disguised as a young man, etc. . . . . p. 34), these include Marthe, Laine's forsaken wife who embodies, we are told, "the passion to serve"; Thomas Pollock Nageoire, "the shrewd American businessman" and Lechy Elbernon, the American actress who represents "the perfidious and multiform desire for freedom" (p. 34).

If we now reconsider, in the light of the play he is about to write, the implications of Claudel's recent statement to Pottecher: "I have sold my freedom and renounced all interests in life,"[6] it seems reasonable to suspect that the real subject of *L'Echange* is what Claudel himself "sold into slavery." That he should be tempted to rebel against the demands of renunciation is not entirely surprising, considering that he is completely uprooted and entirely on his own for the first time and is often lonely, as his letters show.[7]

In *L'Echange*, Claudel, protected by poetic immunity, "buys" back his freedom. He creates Lechy Elbernon, an emancipated, anarchistic, and even sadistic American actress who reflects his own "*désir perfide*," as well as his secret resentment against the divine injunction he has accepted and needs to carry out. The play's dramatic tension arises from Louis Laine's betrayal of his devoted, but possessive, wife—a betrayal which results in his murder by his mistress, Lechy Elbernon.

Claudel has evidently incorporated into this play his first impressions of America.[8] He is not without admiration for Thomas Pollock Nageoire, the American self-made millionaire, the perpetual trader of *L'Echange*, the man who rightly, if rather barbarically, puts a concrete value on all things (see *MI*, 113). He himself, as Henri Guillemin's biographical articles point out bluntly, had a deeply ingrained interest in money, and still remembered, for instance, almost sixty years later, the monthly rental at his New York boarding house (twelve dollars) and the lunches he had to skip for lack of pocket money—a rather humiliating situation for a young bourgeois serving as France's vice-consul in a country where everything seemed to him to have its price in cash.

Marthe's view of the American landscape is dominated by, and serves to express, her own and Claudel's sense of exile and nostalgia for the French landscape:

> *O terre d'exil, tes campagnes me sont ennuyeuses et tes fleuves me paraissent insipides!*

Je me souviendrai de toi, pays d'où je suis venue!
  ô terre qui produit le blé et la grappe mystique!
  et l'alouette s'élève de tes champs, glorifiant
  Dieu.
O soleil de dix heures, et coquelicots qui brillez
  dans les seigles verts! O maison de mon père,
  porte, four!
O doux mal! O odeur des premières violettes qu'on
  cueille après la neige! O vieux jardin où
  dans l'herbe mêlée de feuilles mortes
Les paons picorent des graines de tournesol!
Je me souviendrai de toi ici. (p. 702)

[O land of exile, your countryside bores me and your
  rivers seem to me insipid!
I remember you, country from which I have come! O
  land which produces the corn and the mystical
  grape cluster! And the lark rising from your
  fields, glorifying God.
O mid-morning sun, and poppies which gleam in the
  green rye! O house of my father, door, stove!
O sweet pain! O scent of the first violets gathered
  after the snow! O old garden where, in the
  grass mingled with dead leaves
The peacocks scratch for sunflower seeds!
Here, I remember you.]

It is, however, his other, much more complex existential "exile"
which Claudel is here transposing by deliberately drawing a
depressing image of an American landscape which, in fact, he
often admired, judging from his letters of that period to his
friend, Pottecher.[9]

There are in *L'Echange* three overlapping "exiles" which lend
their tension to the text. There is first Claudel's "exile" from
family life which plunges him into freedom and independence
("I suddenly fell into a life of freedom, from a constricted family
life" *MI*, 116). Secondly, coming to New York with "a religious

training stressing intense fervor and strict asceticism" (*MI*, 78), the poet endures, in the midst of this suddenly acquired freedom, the restricting "exile" of the self-imposed discipline of his faith. Finally, the French Catholic felt exiled because American Catholicism with its "practical and sentimental side . . . did not inspire me much" (*MI*, 98). He is "exiled" from his faith, at least from the familiar French ritual of his faith,[10] at the very time when he still needs to be supported by an elaborate and familiar ritual: "Nothing in the environment sustained me" (*MI*, 99).

It does not take Claudel long to adjust to the absence of his family. As for his nostalgia for France, his ego cures him of it— and not later than the following year. Returning to France in March, 1895, he feels and believes that his literary friends have more or less forgotten him and, as he explains to Amrouche in *Mémoires improvisés*, ". . . after this I no longer, or rarely, felt the sense of nostalgia which Marthe expresses in *L'Echange*" (*MI*, 94).

Lechy Elbernon, the actress, poses intriguing problems. Is she in any sense the transposed figure of some earlier *"partage de midi"* or romantic interlude, or is she the product of an obsessive erotic fantasy?[11] The *Mémoires improvisés*, understandably, shed no light on this problem, but their four chapters on *L'Echange* (XII to XV) provide absorbing commentary on the play as well as a valuable self-portrait. Claudel recalls that as dramatist, his idea while writing the play was "to listen to these four voices [the four characters of the play] and to cooperate with them" (p. 109). In explaining what these voices represent, he recalls that he was beginning to enlarge and shape the philosophical and theological base of his own Catholicism. With the epigraphs to *Le Soulier de Satin* evidently in mind,[12] he reminds Amrouche that "nothing in a human being . . . is contemptible in itself" (p. 107). Ever casting about for "tendencies within Christian doctrine" which may be consistent with his own temperament, Claudel points out that he is "rather in sympathy with the idea of Saint Thomas that everything in human nature is good in it-self; what is bad is the use one makes of it." (*MI*, 108).

He finds "useful" Christian elements in all four characters of *L'Echange*. He finds them in Louis Laine, that restless, adven-turous, rapacious spirit, eager for freedom and ready to "ex-change" his wife for a sum of money. In *Mémoires improvisés*, Claudel speaks of Laine as burning with his own "desire to learn, to know, to embrace all things," and characterizes this desire as a trait which in itself is admirable although, to be sure, it must be guided toward constructive ends (p. 107). In the play, how-ever, Laine is reluctant to bend himself to any purpose, nor is he willing to accept the limitations imposed upon him by mar-riage. Fired by a childlike imagination, he yearns for total "avail-ability": "I should like to be a carpenter . . ./To be the driver of a stagecoach in California" (*Th.* 663); "I should like to be a snake in the luxuriant grass" (p. 665). His self-pitying idleness leaves him perpetually dissatisfied:

> *C'est l'heure où l'ouvrier bâillant remet la courroie*
> *   sur la roue, et le balancier plonge au travers*
> *   du parquet.*
> —*Mais je regarde seulement si je ne trouverai pas un*
> *   lapin avant qu'il rentre au bois ou une dinde*
> *   sur la branche.* (p. 661)

> [This is the time when the yawning worker hooks the
>   belt onto the pulley and the beam plunges
>   through the floor.
> But I am looking only to see if I can find a rabbit
>   before it goes back into the woods or a turkey-
>   hen on a branch.]

Looking about for a symbol to put a Christian stamp on Laine's restless and adventurous spirit, Claudel evokes Saint Francis Xavier setting out to conquer souls and Christianize Asia. In him, too, there burned an adventurous spirit (*MI*, 109). Similarly, Claudel sanctifies the practical side of Thomas Pollock Nageoire,[12] his "yearning to acquire things, which happens to be an aspect of the Christian temperament" (p. 113); his need and habit of putting a cash value on everything: "Is this not simply a primitive and barbaric way of saying things which are true? It is perfectly correct to say that all things have worth and are worth such in terms of our own situation and the use we can make of them" (p. 113). This practical outlook on life, Claudel reminds Amrouche, is not without parallels in Christian doctrine and in the history of Church administration (p. 109).

Even Lechy Elbernon, symbol of perfidious desire, is endowed with solid Christian virtues: "in Saint Francis you find the idea of a slightly wild imagination which carries off the body as on wings, so to speak . . ." (*MI*, 109). Finally, there is Marthe, who also represents "an aspect of the Christian mentality, that sense of family ties and that bourgeois outlook which is undeniably also mine . . ." (p. 109).

The drama itself, Claudel suggests, should be viewed as a human quartet inextricably bound together, the four characters representing aspects of himself in search of unity. The death of Louis Laine should not, he argues, be interpreted as a reflection of the author's desire to eliminate him or his counterpart in himself. For the "idea" he represents remains and continues to play its part in the dynamics of the play. The characters pair off: Marthe, who in the end accepts Pollock's friendship, is not unlike him in their common hatred of waste and their sense of the concrete and practical value of things. Laine and Lechy are evidently destined to seek each other out in a common, reckless and illusory quest for some absolute on earth.

L'Echange has a subtler biographical significance than Claudel is able to recognize, absorbed as he is by the conflicting components of his own image. When Claudel arrives in America in 1893, he already carries in him, so to speak, Marthe, the Christian bourgeoise; Laine, the dreamer and adventurer; and even Thomas Pollock Nageoire—without, to be sure, his *"manière barbare"* of putting actual cash values on everything. The one character of *L'Echange* that is not yet clearly in him, the "original problem" in the play is Lechy Elbernon. Without the Lechy Elbernon-Louis Laine relationship, there is no drama. Their reciprocal interest initiates the action and pulls the other characters tightly around Lechy—as Claudel points out himself "in order to compress Lechy Elbernon" (*MI*, 116). She is a product of the freedom Claudel had never known before 1893 and of the widening horizon of his *"drame intérieur."* He himself views her as a diabolical figure he must learn to cope with, in order to protect his precarious and dangerously threatened equilibrium —an equilibrium dependent on his allegiance to the Church.

And what symbolizes the Church, the suffering mother Church in danger of betrayal, if not Marthe herself? We have here an interesting example of art as instrument of personal salvation. Claudel stages a betrayal of the Church to accomplish a catharsis of his temptation to break his pledge to the Church. Does not Marthe, the faithful wife, burning with what Claudel calls a passion to serve, in the end achieve her intended stature by accepting the "exchange" which generates compassion and charity? In arguing earlier against this exchange and steadfastly clinging to her sacred bond with Louis Laine, her wild husband, does she not act as guardian of and spokesman for Claudel's conscience?

With the very first sentence she utters, in the opening scene, one can sense the tension of Claudel's internal dialogue and detect the dual point of reference implicit in his every contact with the outside world, or, as he prefers to call it, with the Creation: "the day which is clear and which lasts until it is over!" (*Th.* I, 659). The accent is placed at once on the transient and fragile nature of the sensuous world.

For Louis Laine, the night is the moment of face-to-face meeting with the coward in him, the fearful private dialogue with self. He cries to his betrayed wife in the third act: "Tell me that you still love me. The night has come! now I am a coward! now

I can utter these words!" (p. 709). But primitive forces pull him blindly astray ("like the animal/ Towards the hand which feeds him leaves" p. 709)—away from home. And home, implies Marthe, is where the door is safely closed against "the midnight tide . . . with all its noise, crashing against the closed door" (p. 659), where man should come back to sleep.

However, Louis Laine, the American primitive ("I have Indian blood in my veins" p. 662), who wears a shirt of "ox-blood color" is too impetuous and restless to respond to the wisdom of his gentle, European wife, Marthe, domesticated and mellowed by the age-old virtues of her simple faith. His pagan nature is admirably rendered in the description of his morning swim (p. 660).

> *Et je suis sorti de la maison à demi rêvant, riant,*
> *bâillant,*
> *Et je marchais tout nu, et des pins*
> *Les gouttes d'eau me tombaient entre l'oreille et*
> *l'épaule.*
> *Et d'un coup je me suis jeté, la tête en avant,*
> *Dans la mer, telle que le lait nouvellement trait.*
> *Et étant remonté j'ai rendu mon souffle et en même*
> *temps*
> *J'ai vu que le soleil s'était levé, et de nouveau*
> *ayant respiré à plein corps,*
> *Culbutant entre mes genoux, je me suis enfoncé en*
> *bas.*
> *Comme une pierre qui disparaît,*
> *Je descends dans la profondeur de la mer.*
> *Et tantôt je nageais, et tantôt, près du rivage,*
> *me tenant debout, je me passais les mains sur*
> *le corps du haut en bas,*
> *Comme un homme qui se dépouille d'un vêtement.*
> (p. 660)

[And I left the house, half dreaming, laughing,
   yawning,

And I walked completely naked, pine needles
And drops of water fell on my neck.
And swiftly I threw myself, head first,
Into the sea which was like freshly-drawn milk.
And having surfaced, I regained my breath and
    at the same time
Saw that the sun had risen, and again taking
    a deep breath,
I dived down between my knees and plunged to
    the bottom.
Like a stone which sinks from sight
I descended into the depths of the sea.
And at times I swam, and at others, close to
    shore, I stood up and ran my hands the
    whole length of my body
Like a man stripping off his clothes.]

The sun is the symbolic beacon at the center of his world. We are here at the heart of Claudel's conflict with Rimbaud, for insofar as Rimbaud sees himself as "son of the Sun," Claudel knows that he must reject the sun as an illusory god.

Marthe subtly tries to mark the sun as a false idol through the analogy of the lamp removed at night to invite sleep:

> Et le soleil . . . [est] retiré aux hommes comme une
>   lampe,
> Afin qu'ils puissent dormir. (pp. 559-560)

[And the sun is withdrawn from men like a lamp
So that they can sleep.]

Laine, self-absorbed and aloof, replies with an ecstatic ode to the morning sun (p. 661).

When the distraught Laine is challenged by the actress to reveal his infidelity in the presence of his wife, he cries out to Marthe:

O Douce-Amère! Certes, je t'appellerai amère, car
   il est amer de se séparer de toi!
O demeure de paix, toute maturité est en toi!
Je ne puis vivre avec toi, et ici il faut que je
   te quitte, car c'est la dure raison qui le
   veut, et je ne suis pas digne que tu me
   touches.
Et voici que mon secret et ma honte se sont
   découverts!
C'est le corps qui l'a voulu, car il est puissant
   chez les jeunes gens, et il est dur quand il
   tire.
Et il est vrai que j'y ai consenti, et je voulais
   mentir et cacher, mais voilà que cette action
   s'est découverte. (p. 694)

[O Bitter-Sweet! Certainly, I shall call you bitter, for it is bitter to part with you!
O home of peace, all fullness is in you!
I cannot live with you, and here I must leave you,
   for harsh reason demands it, and I am not worthy
   of being touched by you.
And now my secret and my shame are revealed!
It was the flesh which wanted it, for among the young
   it is powerful, and drives hard.
It is true that I consented to it, and wanted to lie
   and hide, but now this act is revealed.]

If Claudel has deliberately drawn, with Marthe, the portrait
of a simple and faithful wife, it is inconceivable that he has done
only that, at this juncture of his spiritual development, as Ernest
Beaumont suggests in *Le Sens de l'amour dans le théâtre de
Claudel.*[13] Betrayed, Marthe grows in stature and rises to the
peak of her eloquence. Her words acquire such resonances as to
reveal her true identity. She pleads her case with the sole purpose
of bringing her lost lamb back to the fold. The fact that she fails
is the clearest sign that Claudel, through Louis Laine, is allow-

ing himself a vicarious experience which consists in giving the pagan side of his nature free play in order to underscore an implicit moral lesson, and to derive from it a beneficial catharsis.

Why would Claudel, whose thoughts at this time are fixed on the problem of renunciation and even on the priesthood,[14] suddenly draw such a character as Marthe and enlist our sympathy for a tender but possessive, uncompromising and protective wife?

> *Laine, j'ai toujours peur pour toi,*
> *Et je pense toujours à toi quand tu n'es pas ici,*
> *Comme à un enfant dont on ne sait ce qu'il fait.*
> *Car, ou vont tes yeux, tes mains y sont bientôt.* (p. 664)

> [Laine, I am constantly afraid for you,
> And I think of you always, when you are not here,
> As one thinks of a child whose whereabouts he does
>   not know.
> For where your eyes go, your hands also are soon
>   there.]

In the years 1893 and 1894, Claudel is still struggling with the staggering demands of his new faith, as his correspondence of that period shows. He is still discovering the self-imposed price he must pay to live not only by the spirit but by the letter of the law, if the joy that lifted his soul at Notre-Dame is to be his to experience again. But he still has a long road to travel before he can hope at least to appease, if not to silence, his "internal debate." For, with Rimbaud, he too, like it or not, is "son of the Sun." And *vis-à-vis* the Church, he is in a difficult situation because what he himself considers forces of evil have a strong claim on his imagination. His portrait of Lechy Elbernon is intended as nothing short of a diabolical figure. As Laine makes his pact with the irresistible but evil freedom she evidently represents for Claudel, he knows he is dying:

Je sais bien que je mourrai bientôt,
Et voici que je t'ai rencontrée comme une touffe de
fleurs funèbres. (p. 699)

[I know full well that I shall soon die,
And here I have met you like a bouquet of funeral
    flowers.]

In the third act, Marthe, speaking for the Church, dictates the
cure:

Mais voici que tu as porté tes pieds de l'autre côté.
Avoue donc ici et confesse-toi.
Tu t'es plongé dans la mer ce matin et tu voulais
    aller jusqu'au fond;
Mais ce n'est pas cette eau salée-là qui te purifiera,
    mais celle qui sort de tes yeux. O Laine, tu es
    vivant encore!
—Donne-moi tes mains! donne-moi tes deux mains!
    (p. 711)

[But now you have gone over to the other side.
Admit it now and confess.
You plunged into the sea this morning and wanted
    to go to the very bottom!
But it is not that salt water which will cleanse
    you, but the water of your own eyes. O Laine
    you are still alive.
Give me your hands! Give me your two hands!]

Earlier, in the first act, Marthe had reminded him of their first
meeting and of their solemn pact—a possible metaphorical allusion to Claudel's sudden conversion:

Et un jour tu es entré chez nous comme un oiseau
Etranger que le vent a emporté.
Et je suis devenue ta femme.

Et voici qu'en moi est entrée la passion de servir.
Et tu m'as ramenée avec toi, et je suis
Avec toi. (p. 665)

[And one day you came among us like an alien
Bird carried in by the wind.
And I became your wife.
And the passion to serve came upon me
And you brought me back with you, and I am with you.]

In the last act, contemplating her husband's dead body, Marthe
recalls his broken pledges:

> *Pourquoi t'es-tu séparé de moi?*
> *Ne m'as-tu pas juré, lorsque tu m'as connue,*
> *Que tu oubliais le monde et que tu avais perdu le*
>   *chemin pour y revenir?*
> *Et moi je t'aimais et je souffrais amèrement entre*
>   *tes mains et je te donnais mon coeur à manger*
> *Comme un fruit où les dents restent enfoncées.*
> *Et voilà que tu m'as quittée comme si je te faisais*
>   *horreur.* (pp. 720-721)

[Why did you cut yourself off from me?
Did you not swear to me, when you met me,
That you would forget the world and that you had
    lost the way back into it?
And I loved you and suffered bitterly in your hands,
    and I gave you my heart to eat
Like a fruit in which the teeth stay sunk.
And then you left me as if I horrified you.]

Claudel has repeatedly pointed out that his creative writing
was one of his most powerful instruments of self-christianization.
L'Echange is no exception. While in America from 1893 to 1894,
he had a great need to lecture himself sternly and, at the same
time, to give full imaginative play to the shadowy dangers sur-

rounding his every step. There seems to be little doubt but that, for the moment at least, the writing of *L'Echange* helped him stay on his chosen path. His ability—common to all true poets— to induce a state of being by the exercise of his artistic talent constitutes the greatest tribute to poetic activity itself. In a practicing but tortured believer, poetry takes on the extended function of substitute prayer, and can create, as Claudel aptly describes it in a letter to Mallarmé, "a state of fictitious felicity" (*Cahiers* I, 44).

NOTES

1 "It seems that before leaving France Claudel wished to 'christianize' [*évangéliser*] his native Tardenois" (Madaule, *Drame*, p. 26).

2 In 1890 Claudel worked in the consular offices in Paris; in the summer of 1892 he vacationed in England, and the following year he was in the United States. See also Pierre Moreau's introduction to the Claudel-Pottecher correspondence (*Cahiers* I, 60-67) and Jean-Claude Berton, "Claudel diplomate" in *Cahiers* IV.

3 Textually the sea, representing the most radical contrast for this earth-bound man: "I am thirsty! I go towards the vastness of the sea!" (p. 510).

4 The text, defective in this respect, does not adequately support and exploit its own hints of a spiritual affinity between Vercors and Violaine.

5 Paul Claudel, *Th.* I, 659-723. On March 11, 1894, Claudel writes to Pottecher from Boston: ". . . the play which I began last spring is finished" (*Cahiers* I, 91).

6 Letter of September 29, 1893, written shortly after Claudel's arrival in New York, (*Cahiers* I, p. 79).

7 His one and only friend, when he prepares to leave the United States in 1894, is the violinist, Laripidie, "*le seul ami que je laisserai en Amérique*" (*Cahiers* I, 95).

8 Sixty years later—after a long diplomatic career which brought him back to the United States as Ambassador—he admits that these early impressions were rather naïve and superficial (*MI*, 93).

9 See especially the letter of January 17, 1894: "I shall miss America and her exquisitely pure skies! Those winter sunrises, that green rising sun suspended over the immaculate snow and the last quarter of the moon at the zenith!"

10 ". . . in France . . . I was constantly exposed to Gregorian chant, the liturgy, Latin. None of this existed in America" (*MI*, 98).

11 The question is not merely indiscreet. Guillemin records, without comment, the fact that Claudel broke his solemn pledge of continence, dating back to December 25, 1890, in the spring of 1893. (See "'La Conversion' de Paul Claudel" in *Etudes Classiques*, Vol. 25, 1957, p. 64.) This coincides with the time when Claudel begins to compose *L'Echange*.

12 The name of Thomas Pollock Nageoire has no symbolic meaning. This can be seen from the amusing way his name was chosen by Claudel (*MI*, 116).

13 "Marthe is perhaps of all the female characters in Claudel, the most realistic in the sense that she represents the ordinary woman solely concerned with domestic life. Her love for her husband is earthy ("She loves her husband in and for himself"); an excellent home maker, she sees no further than her home and her husband's love . . ." [Ernest Beaumont, *Le Sens de l'amour dans le théâtre de Claudel* (Paris: Lettres Modernes, 1958), p. 116].

14 See Chaigne, *Vie*, p. 260; *MI*, 119-125.

CHAPTER IV

From Exile to Poetic Program

One year after writing *L'Echange*, Claudel, now in China[1] composes *Vers d'exil*.[2] These eleven poems reveal that a battle is taking place between God and His ally in Claudel on the one side, and the flesh-and-blood young man on the other—an ambiguous battle ("You have defeated me, my beloved!" [*Tu m'as vaincu, mon bien-aimé!*] *OP*, 18) where welcome defeat opens the door to bliss:

> *Ni le jeune Désir, ni la Raison qui ruse,*
> *Ni la Chimère ainsi qu'un cheval ébloui,*
> *Ne m'ont été loyaux et sûrs! tout m'a trahi!*
> *Et ni mon lâche coeur ne m'a servi d'excuse.*
>
> *J'ai fui en vain: partout j'ai retrouvé la Loi.*
> *Il faut céder enfin! ô porte, il faut admettre*
> *L'hôte; coeur frémissant, il faut subir le maître,*
> *Quelqu'un qui soit en moi plus moi-même que moi.*
>   (p. 18)

[Neither youthful Desire, nor sly Reason
Nor the Chimera like a dazzled horse,
Have been constant, or loyal to me! All have betrayed me!
And my cowardly heart has given me no excuse.

I have fled in vain: everywhere I have found the Law.
I must give up at last! O door, you must admit

54

The guest; trembling heart, you must submit to the
   master,
Someone within me who is more myself than I am.]

In lines reminiscent of Rimbaud's *"combat spirituel,"* Claudel
is fighting both friend and foe, both the inexorable divine injunction:

> *Saisi d'horreur, voici que de nouveau j'entends*
> *L'inexorable appel de la voix merveilleuse.* (p. 13)

[Horror-stricken, again I hear
The inexorable call of the marvellous voice.]

and its enemies in himself. These enemies, most of them familiar
faces, are fully inventoried in *Vers d'exil*:

—The poet's enormous and restless zest for life, that of
   Tête d'Or, of Avare, of Louis Laine, which so far nothing
   has been able to tame (*"Cheval, on t'a en vain mis le
   mors dans la bouche* [Horse, in vain has the bit been
   placed in your mouth]" p. 13);
—His temptation to flee, to escape the relentless call (*"Il
   faut fuir* [I must flee]" p. 13) and the simultaneous awareness of the futility of that escape, as in *L'Echange* (*"J'ai
   fui en vain: partout j'ai retrouvé la Loi* [I have fled in
   vain: everywhere I have met the Law]" p. 18);
—The burden of loneliness and of slavery (*"Rien, retour,
   ne m'accueille, ou départ, me délivre* [Nothing, return,
   greets me, or departure, frees me]" p. 13);
—The intuition, with its attendant anxiety, that he will
   have to chart his own course (*"Nulle route n'est le chemin
   qu'il me faut suivre* [No road is the road I must follow]"
   p. 13) into a future dramatically divorced from the past
   (*"ce lendemain n'est pas du jour qui fut hier* [. . . the
   morrow is not of the day which was yesterday]" p. 13);
—The flesh (*"Car un jour j'ai senti . . ./La réclamation*

de l'entraille profonde [For one day I felt . . ./the demand
of the deep entrail]" p. 14), which is making demands he
may not satisfy ("*Depuis lors je connais le désir sans
douceur* [Since then, I have known desire without re-
lease]" p. 14), etc.

The inventory is rich and could be extended. However, what
is particularly interesting and new in these poems is the complaint, here thinly veiled, there clearly articulated, against God
Himself for inflicting miseries and torments with dictatorial un-
concern, without so much as deigning to give a clear signal, to
speak out, to show His face:

> *Suprêmement assis entre l'âme et le ventre,*
> *Juge sagace avec l'épée et l'examen,*
> *Il enjoint: si je parle, il ne répondra rien,*
> *Mais il faut obéir comme le cercle au centre.* (p. 14)

> [Seated imperially between belly and soul
> Sagacious judge with sword and indictment sheet,
> He enjoins: if I speak, he will not reply,
> But one must obey as the circle does the center.]

Surely this unusually gifted young man, who is being asked
to repress "very important human elements, especially for an
artist: imagination, sensibility, the need for affection . . ." etc.
(*MI*, 121), is entitled to some special mark of God's personal
interest in him: ("*Puisque je suis à toi, découvre-moi ta face!/
. . . . Toi qui m'as appelé, dis-moi ce que tu veux* [Since I am
yours, uncover your face to me/. . . . You who have called me,
tell me what you want]" p. 17).

The daring, the pointed challenge to God, expressed in some
of these poems is matched by a militant buoyancy in which
arrogance conceals desperation:

Et ce qu'un autre a pu obtenir, je le puis.

. . . .

O Dieu, ni devant les hommes, ni devant toi,
Je ne baisserai point les paupières. C'est moi!
C'est moi! Il me faut vaincre ou mourir sur la
    place. (p. 17)

[And what another could obtain, so can I.

. . . .

O God, neither before men, nor before you,
Will I lower my eyes. It is I!
I must conquer or die on the spot.]

The poet even seems to offer God an oblique inducement to
make Him speak out and reveal Himself: he swears ecstatically
that nothing can or ever will deflect him from his course:

Je jure ce soleil que rien ne peut changer
Mon dessein et la route où je chemine et souffre,
Femme, or par terre, feu au loin, détour et gouffre
Et que le pain ne peut paître la faim que j'ai.

Et que tout l'or ne peut combler mon avarice,
Ni l'eau désaltérer ma bouche, ni la mort,
Ni le temps, ni l'éternité finir encor
Mon obsécration, ma joie et mon supplice! (p. 14)[3]

[I swear by this sun that nothing can alter
My purpose or the road I travel, suffering—
Woman, earth's treasure, distant fire, byway, abyss—
That bread cannot allay the hunger that I feel.

And that no gold can satisfy my avarice
No water quench my thirst, nor death,
Time, nor eternity end
My supplication, my torment and my joy.]

There is little doubt that these poems reflect a serious crisis.
These pleas announce a drastic move by Claudel to force and

keep open the door of joy which was threatening to close. Evidently the promised bliss was more demanding of sacrifice than he had expected. It was one thing to impose on Violaine the burden of martyrdom—at relatively little cost to himself and, indeed, with much vicarious satisfaction. But what was Claudel personally prepared to give up besides "frivolous" pleasures—a restraint which could be handsomely repaid by the equally self-indulgent pleasure of pride in abstinence?[4] Does he not stress, in a letter to Jacques Rivière, the sense of superiority which continence creates? What, in short, he began to ask himself, was blocking out the divine light, what was making it so difficult to achieve the necessary internal silence?

The flesh, to be sure, played its part: "The struggle between the flesh and the spirit takes place more or less in every man, at a given moment in his life" (*MI*, 121). But as he was not altogether unsuccessful in making his peace with what he considered transitory and hence illusory pleasures (*Sache, apprends mieux l'ennui de la chose qui passe!* [Know, learn to know well the boredom of whatever passes]" *OP*, 19), he could hardly view his restraint as a sacrifice. And his bliss, he knew, would have to be in direct proportion to his sacrifice ("Happiness is the fruit of sacrifice" *MI*, 138). This could mean only one thing: he would have to make a significant offering and give up—in fact destroy in himself—his most cherished gift, his poetic talent. He would have to give up his poetic vocation.

To leave no doubt as to the magnitude of this sacrifice, Claudel goes to considerable length, in *Mémoires improvisés*, to explain to Jean Amrouche the difference between mere poetic activity and a true poetic vocation:

> . . . a country priest, for instance, who has much free time, and enjoys trying his hand at some poetry, well, it is of no greater consequence than if he turned to carpentry or gardening . . . but the complete and profound attention required in the service of God is incompatible with the

profound attention which a true poet owes to his work . . .
A priest must be entirely priest, from head to toe, and give
everything; if not, if you reserve part of yourself, you are
half and half . . . (*MI*, pp. 153, 155)

In the ensuing discussion, Amrouche raises what is perhaps the
most crucial question in Claudel's life: ". . . what about the
Christian poet, . . . does he not give everything to God?" "Of
course, he doesn't" replies Claudel, ". . . and as Christian he
suffers remorse: when he clearly understands God's demands,
even though he knows that, as Christian poet, he is useful to
others, still he cannot help feeling that he is falling short of the
mark. There is no doubt that the poet will always be inferior
to the saint. There is no comparison between a saint like Saint
Francis and a poet, however distinguished he might be, who
performs on his violin, so to speak, in honor of the glory of
God" (p. 154).

Vers d'exil contains Claudel's first pathetic attempts to destroy
his poetic gift through incantation and verbal exorcism. There
are few more moving pages in Claudel's entire work than these
in which a great poet strives to quiet, stifle and destroy his yet
unborn fictional universe to which, in spite of himself, he will
give life:

> *Bruit de l'homme, pas, cris, rires, appels, devant,*
> *Derrière, chants, amours, rixes, marchés, paroles!*
> *Je te veux aveugler, ô peuple en moi mouvant!*
> *Tais-toi, sonore esprit! Etouffez-vous, voix folles!*
>
> *Bruit de la mer! bruit de la terre! bruit du vent!*
> *Murmure au bois profond, l'oiseau chante. Frivoles*
> *Jours! dors, passé! Que me veux-tu encore, enfant?*
> *Fleur de ce monde-ci, referme tes corolles.*
>
> *Et toi aussi, tais-toi, coeur! taisez-vous, soupir!*
> *Le vieux murmure en moi dure et ne peut finir.*
>
> . . . .
> (*OP*, 16)

[Sounds of men: footsteps, cries, laughs, calls, in front,
Behind, songs, loves, brawls, bargainings, words!
I want you blinded, O people moving within me:
Be silent, sonorous spirit! Stifle yourselves, mad voices.

Sound of the sea! Sound of the earth! Sound of the wind!
Murmurs in the dense woods; the bird sings. Frivolous
Days! Sleep, past! What do you still want of me, child?
Flower of this world, close up again your corollas.

And you also, heart, be silent! Be silent, sigh!
The old murmuring endures in me, and cannot cease.
. . . .]

In the fifth poem Claudel succeeds for a moment in approaching
the serenity he seeks. The voices fall silent, bliss is so close at
hand that his whole being rises, as in a Wagnerian swell, to meet
and receive its reward:

*Tout s'est tu. Viens, ma nuit! Viens-t'en, ombre
    de l'ombre!
Viens, silence sacré et nuptial! Soleil
De mon âme, viens paix! Viens amitié! Viens, nombre!
Viens avec moi, viens, mon Dieu, viens, ardent Sommeil!*
    (p. 16)

[All has grown quiet. Come my night! Come, shade of
    shades!
Come, holy, nuptial silence! Sun
Of my soul, come, peace! Come friendship! Come number!
Come, be with me, my Lord, come, ardent Sleep!]

A year later (1896), still in China, Claudel composes *Le
Repos du Septième Jour*,[5] a theological drama. It represents his
effort to reassess and deepen his understanding of Catholic doctrine in the light of the crisis reflected in *Vers d'exil*. During his
recent home leave in the spring of 1895, his confessor had urged
him to turn to Saint Thomas as an antidote to his despair.[6] The

change of mood, the reaffirmation of faith in *Repos*—in sharp contrast to the pleas, the outcries and the veiled complaints of *Vers d'exil*—suggest that Claudel has found in Saint Thomas powerful arguments against the enemies within. And as he is no longer fighting his battle quite so alone, the *"je"* which occupied the center of the stage in *Vers d'exil* is replaced by an allegorical Chinese emperor, who embodies the spirit of Christian doctrine.

In *Mémoires improvisés*, Amrouche questions the poet about the genesis of the play: "As far as I can remember," explains Claudel, "I wrote this play as an exercise, as a means of exploring both what I was beginning to understand about China and certain theological problems which I wanted to clarify in my mind" (*MI*, 147). Claudel's imagination is captured by what he considers the two salient features of Chinese paganism: the sustained contact with the dead and fear of the devil (*MI*, 148). In the mythical Chinese setting of *Repos*, he confronts the pagan world with Christian doctrine in a pre-Christian *Divine Comedy* which envisions the future christianization of China. The great masses of the suffering Chinese people embody the human condition, groping for a sign (the Cross) that will unlock the mystery of their misery.

Claudel asserts the necessity of self-immolation (represented in the play by the Emperor's willingness to descend into Hell), of purification by fire (symbolized by the leprosy he contracts in Hell), of total self abnegation as man (cf. "Whosoever eats will die" *Th*. I, 809). This grandiose myth of a whole civilization emerging from darkness contains a condensed summary of Christian doctrine. In Madaule's words, "the pilgrimage into the abyss which the Emperor undertakes is necessary preparation for salvation. As the Old Testament is full of prefigurations of the coming of Christ, of his life and passion, similarly, the Emperor of China visits the dead, as did Christ, before the Resurrection, foundation of our faith" (*Drame*, 43).

Characteristically, in the curious hell depicted in the play, Claudel does not fail to put his own stamp on Christian doctrine:

the much-hated scientism of Taine and Renan constitutes one of the capital sins for which a special punishment is reserved in "the circle of Antiscience" (*Th.* I, 832).

The lesson of *Repos* seems to be that man's life on earth is a living death so long as he ignores his debt to God. To repay that debt in full, to reap the highest spiritual reward, he must be able and willing to renounce life. In Christian terms, this is the highest human attainment, synonymous with sainthood. As for the people, they must be protected against the dangers of relapse by a ritual of weekly rededication to God, the "seventh-day rest" or *"repos du septième jour."*

Divided between the call of total renunciation and his poetic vocation, Claudel does not identify himself with the Emperor, but with the rededicated man described in Act II of the play:

> Celui qui est le Principe de Tout, Celui qui est la
>   Cause de Tout en est aussi la Fin.
> C'est pourquoi l'homme composé d'un corps et d'une
>   intelligence
> A été établi son prêtre sur le monde pour qu'il lui
>   en fasse la préparation, l'offrande, le sacrifice
>   et la dédicace,
> Et que, l'ayant reçu dans ses mains, il le lui
>   restitue. (p. 839)

> [He who is the Principle of All Things, He who is
>   the Cause of All is also its End.
> That is why man, made up of a body and an intelli-
>   gence,
> Has been made His priest on earth, in order to pre-
>   pare it for Him, to offer, sacrifice and dedi-
>   cate it to Him,
> And so that, having received it into his hands, he
>   restores it to Him.]

This definition of man's rôle on earth is a prefiguration of Claudel's self-assigned mission, which he will soon state in *Connais-*

sance de l'Est (". . . this world, to which the man endowed with perception and eloquence has been assigned as priest . . ." *OP*, 90). The function of the "priest" will be to participate in and continue the creation. In *La Ville* II, composed one year after *Repos*, Claudel draws a full-fledged portrait of a new Coeuvre, become poet-priest. The self-rededication implicit in the writing of *Repos* is linked to the emergence of Claudel's poetic program, the definition of which was the central preoccupation of *Connaissance de l'Est.*

The fifty-two poems of *Connaissance de l'Est*[7] (1895-1900) give form to a double exploration: that of self and that of the new, fascinating outside world into which Claudel was suddenly plunged when he arrived in China in 1895. Some of the poems contain briefly sketched biographical details that shed a bright or bleak light on the spiritual landscape. He recalls, for instance, his last visit in France with his family:

> *Amère entrevue! comme s'il était permis à quelqu'un*
> *d'étreindre son passé.*
> *C'est ce qui rend le retour plus triste qu'un départ.*
> *Le voyageur rentre chez lui comme un hôte; il est*
> *étranger à tout, et tout lui est étrange.*
> ("*Pensée en Mer*," *OP*, 37-38)

> [Bitter meeting! As if it were given to anyone to
>   embrace his past.
> That is what makes the return sadder than the leav-
>   ing.
> The traveller returns home like a guest; he is alien
>   to everything, and everything is alien to him.]

While gazing at a cemetery, he stresses his own proximity to the living death that seems to be his present life:

J'habite moi-même ce pays de sépultures.
("*Tombes.—Rumeurs*," p. 43)

[I myself live in this land of sepulchres.]

Lonely, apart, he watches in the early morning the poor and homeless of a crowded nation stretched out asleep on the very streets. He ponders, fascinated and envious, the mystery of their nourishing communion with the earth:

> . . . *c'est l'heure où la terre donne à boire et nul*
> *des ses enfants en vain ne s'est repris à son*
> *sein libéral.*
> . . . *voici l'heure où l'homme communique avec sa*
> *mère.* (p. 50)

> [. . . it is the hour when the earth gives of itself
> to drink, and not one of her children comes in
> vain to her generous breast.
> . . . it is the hour when man communes with his mother.]

He hungers for this same nourishing union and sees the moment of awakening as a reluctant weaning:

> *Le dormeur . . . tient au pis et ne lâche point prise,*
> *cette gorgée encore est à lui.* (p. 50)[8]

> [The sleeper . . . clings to the udder, and does not
> let go; this draught, too, is his.]

Walking through a world that could not be more different from the world he knows, Claudel strives to see, to hear, everything and to shape what he experiences into a superbly chiselled prose, worthy of the praise of Mallarmé, whom he unreservedly admired in those years.[9] His poetics are slowly taking form as he finds in the chaotic world he contemplates the same harmony, the same order, the same depth, as in the inner sanctum of a church. Even the landscape sometimes seems a stained-glass window:

> . . . *du haut de la montagne, la plaine avec ses*
> *champs ressemble à un vieux vitrail aux verres*
> *irréguliers enchâssés dans des mailles de plomb.*
> > *("Entrée de la terre,"* p. 44).

> [. . . from high up on the mountain, the plain with
> its fields resembles an old stained glass win-
> dow with irregular glass pieces bound together
> in a web of lead.]

God-like himself, he takes stock of the Creation. Initiating a now famous play on words which he later exploited in *Art Poétique*, to the delight of friends and foes alike, he confidently claims to understand as well as embrace all [*je comprends tout*] (p. 45). He invests the scenery with a spirituality which echoes the inner harmony he yearns to realize. His "descriptions," in which, as Renée Hubert has aptly put it, *"le poète feint mer-veilleusement une soumission à l'objet* [the poet superbly feigns submission to the object]"[10] are rooted in the imagery of his inner world. In *"le Cocotier,"* for example, he notes that

> [*sa*] *cime s'élargissant . . . succombe au poids de*
> *sa liberté.*

> [its crown growing larger . . . succumbs to the
> weight of its liberty.]

Its lower leaves

> *se tiennent affaissées et pendantes, et celles du milieu*
> *s'écartent de chaque côté tant qu'elles peuvent, et celles du*
> *haut, relevées, comme quelqu'un qui ne sait que faire de*

ses mains ou comme un homme qui montre qu'il s'est rendu,
font lentement un signe. (p. 25)

[hang limp, and those in the middle spread out as far as they
can; those at the top stand erect, like someone who does not
know what to do with his hands, or as a man showing that
he has surrendered slowly makes a sign.]

Western trees, he observes, strike a spiritual posture, their
branches reaching out towards the sky like out-stretched arms
(p. 45). Similarly, but in its own way, the branchless coconut
palm, responsive to the earth's muted melody, sways its flexible
trunk in silent harmony with the Creation:

souple, longue, elle [la hampe] est docile au rêve de la
terre. (p. 25)

[supple, long, it (the trunk) responds to the dream of the
earth.]

In December, 1895, Claudel had written to Mallarmé: ". . . I
abhor modern civilization and have always found myself a
stranger to it" (*Cahiers* I, p. 46). The previous year, haunted by
the need of a God that eluded him, he had cried out in *Vers
d'exil:*

Hier! Demain! La chose à faire! tout est fade! Il me dure
et de moi, et de vivre et du jour! (*OP*, 16)

[Yesterday! Tomorrow! The things that must be done!
   Everything is pointless!
I can barely endure myself, life, the day!]

Stopping over in Ceylon, he finds an exotic nature curiously
free of his own anguish and spontaneously making the gracious
gestures his own troubled heart yearns to make:

Et un cocotier, se penchant sur la mer et l'étoile, comme un être accablé d'amour, faisait le geste d'approcher son coeur du feu céleste. (p. 26)

[And a coconut palm, bowing towards sea and star, was gesturing like a being overcome with love, as though to surrender its heart to the celestial fire.]

Claudel laments his exile (". . . the exile he has gone into follows him," p. 38) without, however, striking a tragic note. His real companions are the elements of the Creation with which he constantly identifies:

Que ces eaux sont copieuses! . . . Qu'il est rafraîchissant d'y assortir toutes les nuances de sa peine! (*"Tristesse de l'eau,"* p. 75)

[How copious these waters are! . . . how refreshing it is to read in them all the nuances of one's pain.]

This is not a new element in Claudel. Already at Villeneuve, perched in his apple tree (cf. *"Rêves,"* p. 67), he had felt at home only with nature. This hunger to blend with the Creation now corresponds to his yearning to renounce his poetic talent as a sacrifice to God.

Perhaps the most evidently autobiographical poem in *Connaissance de l'Est* is *"Pensée en Mer,"* the sixth poem of this collection, composed in March, 1896. It recalls, and marks as a turning point, Claudel's loneliness and isolation during his recent home leave in France in the spring of 1895.[11] It records the poet's separation from his past ("This passerby . . . is no longer the same man you took to the fatal quay").

In the deepening conflict between his poetic and religious vocations, two simultaneous but contradictory tendencies can be noted: his exile is becoming increasingly colored by the call of the priesthood, which will reach a critical turning point five years later, at Ligugé, while at the same time, his poetics are clearly taking shape and constitute the major development in *Connaissance de l'Est.* They affirm themselves as a strong counter-current to the solicitations of renunciation, and express, in terms that will no longer change, the axioms of Claudel's artistic vocation. Ironically, he will also find himself "exiled" from his increasingly structured poetics, growing clear in his mind almost in spite of himself. A persistent inner voice urges withdrawal from the world while his will to live presents a counter-proposal to what Claudel calls his "*conseil intérieur,*" or, rather, a compromise proposal. Its object is to combine the rôles of poet and priest, to create, in André Mallet's apt phrase, an Ambassador of God.[12]

In page after page of *Connaissance de l'Est*, and with increasing insistence, Claudel formulates and elaborates his poetics. In "*Tombes.—Rumeurs*" his ear strains to capture the collective and complementary message of blended voices:

> *Chacun croit qu'il parle seul. . . . Mais sa parole ne périt pas: elle porte, de l'innombrable addition de la voix collective où elle participe. . . . Or, comme il y a un mélange entre les sons, se fait-il une communication entre les sens . . .* (pp. 43-44)

> [Everyone believes that he speaks alone. . . . But his words do not perish: they resound augmented by innumerable additions of the collective voice in which they participate. . . . Now, as there is a mingling of sounds, so a communication between meanings is achieved.]

In "*Peinture,*" assuming his rôle of "census taker of the earth," he proposes to paint our globe with its myriad details:

> *Que l'on me fixe par les quatre coins cette pièce de soie . . . d'un bord jusqu'à l'autre, comme entre de nouveaux horizons, d'une main rustique j'y peindrai la terre. Les limites des communes, les divisions des champs y seront exactement*

dessinées, ceux qui sont déjà en labour, ceux où demeure debout le bataillon des gerbes encore. Aucun arbre ne manquera au compte, la plus petite maison y sera représentée avec une naïve industrie. (p. 55)

[Let someone fasten a piece of silk for me by its four corners. . . . From one edge to the other, as between new horizons, I will paint the earth with a primitive hand. The boundaries of communes and the divisions of the fields will be drawn there exactly—those already being worked, those where the battalions of the sheaves of corn are still standing. Not a single tree will be missing from the account, the smallest house will be represented with a naïve industry.]

In *"La Dérivation,"* laying the foundation for a subsequent development in *"La Muse qui est la Grâce,"* the poet defines his artistic objective in a striking formula: *"Jouir, c'est comprendre, et comprendre, c'est compter* [Bliss is understanding, and to understand is to count]" (p. 60).[13] In *"Le Fleuve* [The River],"* anticipating *"L'Esprit et l'Eau"* (1906), he gives to the word "water" some of the symbolic meanings it will have in the second Ode, identifying the river with the bloodstream:

celle-ci fait appel à ce qu'il y a en nous entre la chair et l'âme, notre eau humaine chargée de vertu et d'esprit, le brûlant sang obscur. Voici l'une des grandes veines ouvrières du monde, l'un des troncs de distribution de la vie, je sens marcher sous moi le plasma qui travaille et qui détruit, qui charrie et qui façonne. (p. 62)

[. . . this (river) reflects what we have in us between the flesh and the soul, our human water charged with virtue and spirit, the burning dark blood. This is one of the great working arteries of the world, one of the branches of the distribution of life; I feel flowing under me the plasma which works and which destroys, which bears away and builds up.]

"*La Nuit à la vérandah*" foreshadows the cosmic role Urania will play in "*Les Muses:*"[14]

> *La position des astres n'est point livrée au hasard; le jeu de leurs distances me donne les proportions de l'abîme, leur branle participe à notre équilibre, vital plutôt que mécanique. Je les tâte du pied.* (p. 64)

[The position of the stars is not left to chance; the interplay of their distances gives me the proportions of the abyss, their movement plays a part in our balance, vital rather than mechanical. My foot can reach out and touch them.]

"*La Cloche,*" the haunting anecdote of the frustrated bell maker, dramatizes Claudel's own dilemma by stressing that art (like the priesthood) requires a total gift of self:

> *Et il voulut, cette fois, dans la poche d'un profond vaisseau, recuellir l'âme et le bruit entier de la Terre nourricière et productrice, et ramasser dans un seul coup de tonnerre la plénitude de tout son. Tel fut le dessein qu'il conçut; et le jour qu'il en commença l'entreprise, une fille lui naquit.*
>
> *Quinze ans il travailla à son oeuvre. Mais c'est en vain qu'ayant conçu sa cloche il en fixa avec un art subtil les dimensions et le galbe et le calibre; . . . son angoisse était de ne point sentir là la vie et ce je ne sais quoi de moelleux et d'humide conféré par la salive aux mots que forme la bouche humaine.*
>
> .   .   .   .
>
> *Alors une grande pitié naquit dans le coeur de la vierge, pour laquelle aujourd'hui les femmes viennent, près de la cloche, vénérer sa face de bois peint. Ayant fait sa prière au dieu souterrain, elle vêtit le costume de noces, et, comme une victime dévouée, s'étant noué un brin de paille autour de cou, elle se précipita dans le métal en fusion.*
>
> *C'est ainsi qu'à la cloche fut donnée une âme. . . .* (p. 71)

[And he wanted, this time, to gather the soul and all the clangor of the nourishing and productive earth, into the cavity of a large vessel and to amass the fullness of all sound in a single clap of thunder. Such was the aim he conceived, and the day on which he began the enterprise, a daughter was born to him.

For fifteen years he worked at his task. But it was in vain that, having conceived his bell, he fixed with subtle artistry, the dimensions, contours and diameter; . . . his anguish lay in the feeling that life was not in it nor that damp and humid *je ne sais quoi* which saliva confers upon the words formed by the human mouth.

. . . .

Then a great compassion was born in the heart of the virgin for whose sake, today, the women come to the bell, to venerate her face of painted wood. Having said a prayer to the God of the nether world, she put on a wedding gown, and, like a sacrificial victim, after tying a piece of straw around her neck, she plunged into the molten metal.

In this way the bell was given a soul. . . .]

Perhaps the poem which most clearly shows that Claudel has now formulated his poetics, and in terms which will often recur later, is "*Le Promeneur:*"

Chaque arbre a sa personnalité, chaque bestiole son rôle, chaque voix sa place dans la symphonie; comme on dit que l'on comprend la musique, je comprends la nature, comme un récit bien détaillé qui ne serait fait que de noms propres; au fur de la marche et du jour, je m'avance parmi le développement de la doctrine. Jadis, j'ai découvert avec délice que toutes les choses existent dans un certain accord, et maintenant cette secrète parenté par qui la noirceur de ce pin épouse là-bas la claire verdure de ces érables, c'est mon regard seul qui l'avère, et, restituant le dessein antérieur, ma visite, je la nomme une révision. Je suis l'Inspecteur de la Création, le Vérificateur de la chose présente; la solidité de ce monde est la matière de ma béatitude! (pp. 84-85)[15]

[Each tree has its personality, each little beast its rôle, each voice its part in the symphony; as one speaks of understanding music, so I understand nature, like a very detailed narration which would be composed of only proper names; as the journey and the day proceed, I move deeper into the ramifications of the doctrine. Once, I discovered with delight that all things exist in a certain harmony, and now it is my glance alone which establishes this secret relationship by which the blackness of the pine down there is wedded to the bright greenness of these maples, and, restoring the former design, my visit, I call it a review. I am the Inspector of the Creation, the Verifier of things present; the solidity of this world is the substance of my beatitude.]

In *Connaissance de l'Est* Claudel's theory of speech as a manifestation of the divine in man and his concept of the poet-priest are linked for the first time (paralleling Coeuvre's evolution into a poet-priest in the second version of *La Ville*):

. . . la parole . . . implique, restitution intelligible du souffle, l'aveu. Puisque chaque créature née de l'impression de l'unité divine sur la matière indéterminée est l'aveu même qu'elle fait à son créateur, et l'expression du Néant d'où il l'a tirée. Tel est le rythme respiratoire et vital de ce monde, dont l'homme doué de conscience et de parole a été institué le prêtre pour en faire la dédicace et l'offrande, et de son néant propre uni à la grâce essentielle, par le don filial de soi-même, par une préférence amoureuse et conjugale. ("*Ça et là,*" *OP*, 90)

[. . . the word . . . implies intelligible restoration of the breath, avowal. Since every creature born of the impress of the divine unity on indeterminate matter *is* the avowal itself which it *makes* to its Creator, and the *expression* of the

Nothingness out of which He has drawn it. Such is the breathing and vital rhythm of this world, of which man, endowed with consciousness and speech, has been ordained priest, to make the dedication and offering of it and from his own nothingness united with essential grace, by the filial gift of himself, by a loving and conjugal choice.]

The poems Claudel wrote following his visit to Japan repeat his poetics in the minor key of art criticism. He is absorbed by them and stresses in Japanese art what corresponds to his own preoccupation:

L'artiste européen copie *la nature selon le sentiment qu'il en a, le Japonais l'imite selon les moyens qu'il lui emprunte . . . l'un reproduit dans son détail le spectacle qu'il envisage d'un oeil probe et subtil; l'autre dégage d'un clignement d'oeil la loi, et, dans la liberté de sa fantaisie, l'applique, avec une concision scripturale.* ("Ça et là," p. 86)

[The European artist *copies* nature according to the feeling he has for it; the Japanese *imitates* it in accordance with the means he borrows from it . . . the former reproduces in all its detail the spectacle which he envisions with a steady and subtle eye; the latter, with the blink of an eye, extracts the law from it, and in the freedom of his fancy, applies it with scriptural conciseness.]

In the remaining eleven poems of *Connaissance de l'Est* (from "*Le Sédentaire*," p. 91 to "*La Terre quittée*," p. 106), Claudel's poetics and his mission as artist continue to be his main concern. In "*Salutation*" he again defines his artistic objective as he salutes the earth:

Et je saluerai cette terre, non point avec un jet frivole de paroles inventées, mais en moi que la découverte soudain d'un immense discours cerne le pied des monts comme une mer d'épis traversée d'un triple fleuve. Je remplis, comme

un plaine et ses chemins, le compartiment des montagnes.
Tous les yeux levés vers les montagnes éternelles, je salue
populeusement le corps vénérable de la Terre. (p. 94)

[And I will salute this earth, not with a frivolous spurt of
invented words, but in me may the sudden discovery of an
immense utterance encircle the foot of the mountains like a
wheatfield crossed by a threefold river. I fill, like a plain
and its roads, the division between the mountains. All eyes
raised toward the eternal mountains, I multitudinously
salute the venerable body of the Earth.]

"La Source" combines in one powerful image his artistic and
spiritual goals against a background of *"mépris"* for modern
society:

Et je découvre dans un creux la source. Comme le grain
hors du furieux blutoir, l'eau de dessous la terre éclate à
saut et à bouillons. La corruption absorbe; ce qui est pur
seul, l'original et l'immédiat jaillit. Née de la rosée du ciel,
recueillie dans quelque profonde matrice, l'eau vierge de
vive force s'ouvre issue comme un cri. Heureux de qui une
parole nouvelle jaillit avec violence! Que ma bouche soit
pareille à celle de cette source toujours pleine, qui naît là
d'une naissance perpétuelle toute seule, insoucieuse de servir
aux travaux des hommes et de ces bas lieux où, nappe
épandue, mélangée comme une salive à la boue, elle nourrira
la vaste moisson stagnante.

[And in a hollow I discover the spring. The water bursts
from under the ground, spurting and seething like grain
from the whirling mill. The corrupt is absorbed; only what
is pure, the original and the immediate, gushes up. Born
of the dew of the heavens, gathered in some deep womb,
the virgin water springs forth mightily like a cry. Happy
is he from whom a new word violently springs. May my
mouth be like the perpetually filled spring's which is born
there of a perpetual and solitary birth, not concerned with

serving the works of men, and those low places where, spread, mixed like saliva with mud, it will nourish the vast stagnant harvest.]

As Claudel's first China assignment draws to a close, he is evidently fascinated by his own poetics. In fact, he is obsessed by them in self-defense, to counterweigh his need to renounce his art and withdraw from the world.

During the same period (1895-1900), Claudel reshapes *La Ville* and *La Jeune fille Violaine* with the new insights attained during the composition of *Connaissance de l'Est*. In *La Ville* II (1897) he incorporates some of his recent reflections on art and enlarges the rôle of Coeuvre to include the functions of priest, in line with his now sharply defined poetics. *Violaine* II (1898) also reflects aspects of the emerging poetics, enriching the renunciation theme. Pierre de Craon, the master church builder introduced for the first time in this version of the play, adds an esthetic dimension to the mystical message of the original version. Twelve years later, in *L'Annonce faite à Marie* (1910)— the third version of *La Jeune fille Violaine*—Claudel carries his present efforts to their logical goal: he successfully orchestrates the themes of the "artist-priest" (represented by Pierre de Craon) and the true saint (Violaine, now identified with the Virgin Mary). By then he is able to view the esthetic requirements of his subject "from the outside," as he recognizes in *Mémoires improvisés* (p. 51) since he has abandoned his own quest for sainthood.

NOTES

1 In February, 1895, Claudel travels back to France on home leave. In July, 1895, he arrives in Shanghai. See *Cahiers Paul Claudel*, IV, "*Claudel Diplomate*," 99-116. This volume contains the most reliable information available on Claudel's movements in the course of his diplomatic career.

2 Paul Claudel, *OP*, 13-20. These poems were written in Shanghai, in 1895. See *MI*, 123: "All these poems were written at the same time. I had just arrived in Shanghai; I remember that I was in a hotel room when I wrote them."

3 How Claudel could have viewed these poems as a mere exercise in verse writing is almost beyond comprehension. (See *Cahiers* I, p. 98). One can only assume that to maintain his own equilibrium, he could not afford to understand fully what he was doing. The same will be true later at Ligugé.

4 *Jacques Rivière et Paul Claudel: Correspondance (1907-1914)*, p. 24. (Letter of March 3, 1907) .

5 Paul Claudel, *Th.* I, 797-860.

6 Chaigne, *Vie*, p. 68.

7 Paul Claudel, *OP*, 23-107.

8 It is passages such as these, and especially one reference in *Violaine* to a bitter weaning experience, that have led Weber to make Claudel's complete works derive from a traumatic weaning experience in the poet's life.

9 See the Claudel-Mallarmé correspondence of this period in *Cahiers* I, 17-39.

10 R. R. Hubert, "Claudel, poète en prose," *French Review*, February, 1962, p. 372.

11 See Claudel's comments on this poem in *MI*, 95-96 and 120. The composition date of March, 1896, seems justified on the grounds that:

    1) in the poem the poet is recalling his home leave of the previous year (the only leave he has had so far): "*La pensée du voyageur se reporte à l'année précédente. . . . On allait lui remontrer les parents, les amis, les lieux, etc. . . .* [The traveller's thoughts return to the preceding year. . . . He was going to revisit his parents, friends, places . . .]" *OP*, 37);

    2) Claudel has written a great deal at sea and there is no reason to assume that this was not the case here ("*Le bateau fait sa route entre les îles, etc.*, [The boat makes its way through the islands.]" p. 37) ;

    3) in March of 1896 Claudel was transferred from Shanghai to Foochow and must have travelled to his new post by boat, sailing between the coastal islands of the China Sea.

12 See Robert Mallet's introduction to *André Suarès et Paul Claudel: Correspondance*, p. 13.

13 This statement, which presents Claudel as "census-taker" of the Creation, offers a clear contrast with Gide, who in exactly the same period seeks in knowledge the courage to be himself: "*Comprendre, c'est se sentir capable de faire*, [To understand is to feel oneself capable of doing.]" *Les Nourritures terrestres, Oeuvres complètes* (Paris: Gallimard, 1933) , II, 67.

14 Cf. "*Les Muses*," *OP*, 227.

15 This concept of the complementary rôle of colors in expressing universal harmony is illustrated, at about the same time, by the poet Coeuvre in *La Ville* II (1897):

> *O Besme, si cette feuille devient jaune,*
> *Ce n'est point parce que la terre occupe telle*
>   *position sur son orbite, ce n'est point*
>   *parce que les canaux obstrués se flétrissent,*
> *Et ce n'est point non plus pour que, tombant, elle*
>   *abrite et nourrisse au pied de l'arbre les*
>   *graines et les insectes.*
> *Elle jaunit pour fournir saintement à la feuille*
>   *voisine qui est rouge l'accord de la note*
>   *nécessaire. (Th.* I, 427)

> [O Besme, if this leaf becomes yellow,
> It is not because the earth is at a particular
>   point in its orbit, it is not because the
>   choked veins are withering,
> And neither is it in order that, falling, it may
>   nourish and shelter the insects and seeds at
>   the foot of the tree.
> It yellows in order to piously furnish the neighboring
> leaf which is red the note necessary for harmony.]

CHAPTER V

The Poetic Program vs. The Religious Vocation

Between 1897 and 1900 Claudel is increasingly preoccupied with the conflict inherent in his two vocations. The poetic program he has been formulating—almost in spite of himself—serves to increase the tension between his mutually exclusive options: to serve God in the world as poet, or to withdraw from the world. A turning point is approaching, for in 1900 he is due back in France on home leave, and will then have to decide whether to accept a new diplomatic assignment: "What awaits me, what shall I do when I return to France? Shall I try monastic life?" he recalls asking himself repeatedly—a painful, "throbbing" thought (*"une pensée lancinante"*), "which was underlying all my artistic work of this period. . . ." (*MI*, 121).

In this connection, it cannot be overemphasized that Claudel's diplomatic career is in no way directly involved in this conflict of vocations. To be sure, in order to withdraw from the world he would have to resign from the Foreign Service, but his inner turmoil does not stem from the conflict of diplomatic career *vs.* monastic life, as one recent critic has suggested. To assume that it does is to identify Claudel too closely with Mesa, his counterpart in *Partage de Midi*. Mesa too is a civil servant, but he is not a poet[1]—and it is the poet, not the diplomat, who is threatened by the conflict of vocations.

There is evidence that as early as 1898 Claudel is attempting to resolve this conflict in favor of withdrawal by a determined effort to restrain his lyricism, to silence his imagination, to

77

anaesthetize his sensibility. Some of the last poems of *Connais-sance de l'Est*, for instance (*"Proposition sur la lumière*," *"Sur la cervelle"*), are pretentiously scholastic and aridly expository. The pieces on Japan, inspired by his visit to that country in June, 1898, border on the essay, with a bare minimum of poetic effect.

In a letter to Francis Jammes dated June 28, 1898,[2] Claudel acknowledges this tendency towards a more arid prose. Commenting on Jammes's *"De l'Angélus de l'Aube à l'Angélus du Soir,"* Claudel writes admiringly: Your poem made me understand "how argumentative and dry I have become."[3] In this same letter, and without a trace of regret, Claudel appears to bid farewell to literature; thanking his friend for praising his "imperfect and ridiculous works," a compliment which "in earlier years would have pleased me more," he adds with solemnity: "The illusory character of the dream which I was pursuing, by means of literature, no longer escapes me" (*Corresp.* Cl./Jam./Friz., p. 26). His correspondence with Jammes and others during this period reflects his persistent absorption with literature, however, betrayed in fact by the very flourish with which he asserts his wish to renounce it.

In a letter to Pottecher, probably written in 1899, the poet takes his friend vigorously to task for his interest in popular theater and his prosaic conception of the dramatist's rôle in society. Forcefully, he defines his own concept, rooted in ancient tragedy.[4] Furthermore—and this shows what a difficult year 1899 must have been for him, drawn as he is in opposite directions, waging battle on all fronts—he lambastes Jammes in a letter dated February 12, 1899, for sneering at asceticism in the following passage of *"Prière pour se recueillir,"* one of the poems in *Quatorze prières*, which Jammes had recently published:[5]

> *Je ne porterai point de corde autour des reins:*
> *car c'est insulter Dieu que de meurtrir la chair.*

Amant des prostituées et des fiancées claires,
mon coeur chante à la femme un angélus sans fin.

Je n'admirerai point celles aux fauves bures,
car c'est nous voiler Dieu que voiler la beauté:
mais je veux que la vierge aux seins dressés et durs
fleurisse comme un lis à l'azur fiancé.

[I will not bind up my loins with cords:
for it is an insult to God to punish the flesh.
Lover of whores and delicate fiancées,
my heart sings to woman a ceaseless angelus.

I will not admire those who wear brown sackcloth,
for to veil beauty is to veil God from us:
but I want the virgin with the firm up-pointed breasts
to flower like a lily affianced to the sky.]

Shocked by these two strophes deriding the very monastic ideal he was making ready to accept, Claudel attacks Jammes in no uncertain terms, betraying by his eloquent irritation the pertinence of monastic withdrawal to his private drama. He asks his friend bluntly what prompted him to sneer at asceticism; he wonders how a mind as free as his from the commonplace ("*un esprit si peu conventionnel*") does not understand that asceticism is as natural to man as other vital instincts; he is baffled and hurt by Jammes's contempt for those who embrace monastic life as the best means of expression for the primordial ascetic instinct. Barely controlling his anger, he asks solemnly:

How could you possibly have written: 'it is an insult to God to punish the flesh'? I cannot forgive you this superficiality, worthy of romanticism and naturalism. 'The glorification of the flesh' or rather of the sexual act was invented by writers. . . . At night—and for reasons buried deeply in the human heart—a gloomy funereal reserve [*une pudeur funèbre*], the sinner's bitter, penitential sorrow [*l'amertume*

pénitentielle] ever attend the union of man and woman.
. . . But sacred bliss, endless, spiritual strength [*la ressource éternelle*], divine and inexhaustible joy—these cannot be found in the arms of a woman. (*Corresp.* Cl./Jam./Friz., pp. 27-28)

In spite of all his declarations to the contrary, Claudel remains throughout this difficult period, and up to his retreat at the monastery of Ligugé, the inveterate man of letters he will be all his life, to his professed embarrassment, frustration and regret. In August 1899, he receives his first letter from Gide and two of his books, *Le Prométhée mal enchaîné* and *Philoctète ou le Traité des trois Morales*. These books, and especially their author's mind fascinate the would-be priest, as does the magic of Gide's style which he studies with great curiosity and characterizes with keen perception: "Your mind has not a single slant [*votre esprit est sans pente*]" he tells Gide. "I have studied your style with great pleasure: the words and phrases come together [*s'assemblent*] not for reasons of logic or harmony, but by a sort of moist attraction, a kind of secret circulation which animates the whole work and seems to make the entire book the metamorphosis of a self-same word."[6]

Claudel leaves China in October 1899, and undertakes a disappointing pilgrimage to the Holy Land[7] before returning to France where he spends about six months, from April to mid-October, 1900. Shortly after his arrival in France, he travels through the countryside, stopping to look at churches, and begins an essay on church architecture, ambiguously entitled, "*Développement de l'Eglise.*"[8] He meets Francis Jammes—their first meeting and the only one that year—in the presence of André Gide and Marcel Schwob and tells a startled Jammes that he does not quite see in him "a man with a religious and Catholic cast of mind" (*Corresp.* Cl./Jam./Friz., p. 29).[9] Soon afterwards, in a letter to Jammes dated May 8, 1900, he tries to explain and to some extent attenuate this criticism.

This letter, written less than three months before Claudel's retreat at the Abbey of Solesmes, shows Claudel bracing himself to resemble the man he must become if he is to withdraw successfully from the world. He sets the tone at once by alluding to "these moments when one feels most desperately alone and confined [*séquestré*], as for instance, when "one is in the world" (p. 28).[10] What disturbs him in Jammes is an over-abundance of tenderness, of sensibility, and of what he calls accessibility of heart (p. 29). He finds this sentiment incompatible with Catholicism ("Catholicism is a marvellously narrow, jealous and intolerant doctrine!"), incompatible also with the wisdom he seeks ("Any sensation we have of which [Catholic doctrine] does not approve and which it cannot therefore share, so to speak, grieves our inner wisdom—ever present as a nagging, insufferable wife. . . ." p. 29). While holding up impervious callousness as a lofty goal ("Your garden is not closed but open"), Claudel concedes to having too much sensibility himself and to responding only too well to pathetic situations; but he finds the resulting tenderness a source of irritation (p. 29). In a vigorous conclusion, he condemns all forms of warmth and tenderness which, when fanned, cannot "become a flame and . . . serve to forge our soul into a key!" (p. 29).

Carried away in this letter by the double-purpose exorcism of his own eloquence, intended to channel both Jammes and himself in the right direction, Claudel suddenly feels a little ridiculous and, in closing, undercuts his own words by breaking into a chuckle:

Incidentally, take all this with a grain of salt. I try as best I can to make myself understood and have no wish to take a doctoral tone with you. (When I look at myself in the mirror to shave, there are times when I think I begin to resemble the high-priest Caiaphas or Bishop Cauchon: the only thing missing is the fur-fringed vestment! . . .) (*Corresp.* Cl./Jam./Friz., p. 29)

He could not have written a more fitting conclusion to a fictitious self-portrait: as one steps back a bit, one sees the mirror's frame which destroys the illusion of reality.

The last time Claudel writes to Jammes, before returning to China that year, is on August 12, 1900. His letter, written at the most a few days before he goes into retreat at the Benedictine abbey of Solesmes, shows him still very much concerned with matters of literature, and even deploring his failings as poet. The pretext at hand happens to be a letter from Jammes dealing with *L'Echange*, which Jammes had just read in *L'Ermitage*.[11] Pleased by Jammes's flattering comments and satisfied that his friend has understood the play perfectly,[12] Claudel criticizes what he calls his own deplorable jumble (*"ce triste galimatias"* p. 30) and the "eruptive" character of his style. He goes on to characterize the true poet he evidently would like to be: "I feel that the work of a true poet ought to render everything 'intelligible,' I mean deliciously soluble; that literature ought to 'find the word' for all things [*trouver le mot de tout*]" (p. 30). He describes his own artistic activity as but a means in his quest for serenity: "My plays have never been anything but more or less elaborate devices to allow my inner debate to talk itself out . . ." (p. 30).

The internal debate has not so far resolved the conflict of vocations, however. Instead, it has led the poet into an impasse. The next step for Claudel is to tear out his poet's heart, blind himself to the outside world and test his capacity for sainthood. Some deserve to be reached directly by God, he writes with a hint of envy a quarter of a century later in *Le Soulier de Satin* (*Th.* II, 807), the Divine Spirit reaching the human spirit as on a straight line; others have to be reached in less direct ways. By late summer of 1900, the time had come for Claudel to try breaking out of his spiritual conflict by testing the straight line.

Why he had not done so before the completion of his tour of duty in China is due, in part, to his ingrained bourgeois reflex, to his civil servant's or *"fonctionnaire"* 's conscience, long a family tradition. But it also reflects to a considerable extent his reluctance to force the issue, as well as his inability to disappear quietly, to dedicate himself entirely, in simple anonymity, to the service and adoration of God.

His attempted withdrawal takes place in full view of his public: "a complete but ostentatious sacrifice," he admits in 1948, "in which my self-esteem found subtle compensations" (*OC*, XI, 305). This public is the small but thoroughly informed avant-garde world of French letters. His retreats are the famous and much patronized abbeys of Solesmes and Ligugé, where prominent Christian writers occasionally made a moderately purifying withdrawal, prior to returning, braced and refreshed, to the exciting world of letters.

At Ligugé, his half-hearted bid for sainthood is rejected. Claudel will never forget that at this critical juncture in his life, he failed to make what he calls "class A": "I felt," he explains in *Mémoires improvisés*, "that I had been relegated forever to class B . . ." (p. 156). In his frame of reference, class A is reserved for those who renounce everything, even God's gifts; it is they who are the only true saints. Claudel's hunger for sainthood is so strong that during his radio interviews with Amrouche, and oblivious of his audience, he movingly stops to reappraise the still painful experience, now fifty years old, of his unsuccessful attempt to become a monk. He wonders out loud, in a pathetic and somewhat confused self-examination, whether God would have rejected him if indeed he had been a saint; or, on the other hand, whether he might not have become one by forcing God's hand, so to speak: "Yes, . . . I have had the impression that I did not make a maximum effort; what might have happened . . . it is not entirely impossible: had I really been a saint or a hero, who knows whether I would not have overlooked God's rejection of me, and if I might not after all have been truly a saint?" (p. 157).

To "do the maximum," in this context, can mean only one thing: to give up the poetic vocation. But that is precisely what

Claudel did not and could not do, and the most dramatic proof of it is that while at Solesmes and Ligugé he wrote one of his most famous poems, "*Les Muses*." This poem inflicts on the cause of renunciation a most devastating defeat; and not only because of its content, as we shall see, but also, and perhaps especially, because it was written at all.

What really did happen during Claudel's unsuccessful retreat? In early August of 1900 he went to Solesmes, where he remained at most a few weeks. This retreat was interrupted by trips to Paris to consult his regular confessor, the Abbé Villaume, evidently to arrange for his admission as novice at Ligugé. On September 9 the Abbé wrote to Cardinal Richard, Archbishop of Paris, to request an audience for Claudel "who is giving up, at the age of 32, a brilliant career to enter soon the Benedictine order of Ligugé."[13] His retreat at Ligugé must have taken place in late September or early October for he sailed back to China in the last week of October.

According to Chaigne, Claudel remained exactly eight days at Ligugé.[14] It was indeed a lively place, full of "writers and artists" (Chaigne, p. 82). He met Louis Le Cardonnel, whose heroic efforts to renounce the world were to fail; he met Huysmans who was staying at La maison Notre-Dame. Claudel's spiritual counselor was Dom Besse, a Benedictine monk of singular vigor, wisdom and perception, who took charge of him and studied his case "with his rare gift for recognizing true religious commitment, for which he was well known and because of which he had been put in charge of the novices" (p. 83). Claudel was advised that he would better serve the Church by remaining "in the world."

In an important letter to Louis Massignon (dated November 19, 1908, quoted by Chaigne, p. 84), Claudel comments on this dramatic story. It appears that his spiritual Superiors at Ligugé, concerned about the deteriorating political situation in China, ordered him to postpone his retreat and go back to China:

". . . my Superiors ordered me to wait, because of the political situation [the Boxer rebellion] and to return to China." "It is probable," adds Claudel with moving sincerity, "that if I had insisted on staying at Ligugé, I could have remained, but my heart was not in it . . . the sacrifice . . . was above my strength." In *Mémoires improvisés* he relates these same events and reports being advised by his *"supérieurs"*[sic][15] to return to China. The motives he gives, however, are different: they sent him back to further test his faith: ". . . *pour m'éprouver davantage*" (p. 151).

Certain important details of these events remain curiously shrouded in mystery. For instance, why did Claudel, who in early August had gone to Solesmes for an extended and decisive retreat, move to Ligugé in September or early October? Louis Chaigne, who seems to know the details of Claudel's contacts with the Catholic clergy in France, admits in his biography of the poet that this point is not yet clear (p. 82). Claudel is himself responsible for the confusion surrounding this pivotal moment in his life. He has made allusions to this event which even Chaigne, his most fervent hagiographer, is forced to admit are conflicting: "If the decision [of his advisers] is clear, the various circumstances described by Claudel conflict in matters of detail. As for what he was told, did he not already know that there was no better solution for him, whatever the cost?" (p. 85, n.61).

Apparently not. In fact Claudel was quite unaware of the outcome he was really hoping for, as his most extensive account of this episode shows:

It was a great tragedy for me because a sacrifice such as I had made cannot be repeated in a lifetime. I remember that when I was advised not to pursue the matter, I went up into the chapel reserved for the novices at Ligugé and stayed there, very perplexed, trying to decide what to do. Then I received a very clear, categorical and perfectly simple answer: *no*. No other commentary, just that, a pure and simple no, as clear as could be. No alternative was offered: simply

no. I just couldn't, the road was blocked. . . . Naturally, I
tried to argue. I was not yet entirely convinced . . . (*MI*,
151).

He was so hesitant as to what he should do that he even consulted
his mother—the only time on record—who wisely asked him to
wait another year and also urged his return to China (Chaigne,
Vie, p. 83).

Bracing himself for a further testing of his faith, Claudel then
breaks with the world of letters in a farewell note to Pottecher
(October 12, 1900):

> I am leaving this Friday and returning to Foochow. This is
> the last letter you will receive from me. Henceforth I shall
> be silent for a long time, perhaps forever.

Pottecher's acknowledgment of that letter has not thus far been
published, but the first draft of his reply, written at Meudon
on October 24, 1900, has turned up. In it, he salutes his friend's
artistic talent and urges him not to abandon literature. In a wish
that reads like a prophecy, he hopes that the Muses, even against
Claudel's own will, will earn and successfully defend their right
to speak:

> If you are silent with me, do not at least be silent in your
> art; do not smother the dark daemon full of lightning which
> I have recognized in you and hailed. May he be stronger
> than your very will and disobey you if you should order
> him to be silent forever. (*Cahiers*, I, 110)

Claudel paid dearly for the adventure of Ligugé, where in
effect he had attempted to bargain with God, so to speak. Let
sainthood be granted me, he seems to have said to God, and I
shall then sacrifice my art—in that order. His subsequent moral
collapse and his suffering make him see through his self-deception:

Parce que je Vous ai aimé
Comme on aime l'or beau à voir ou un fruit, mais alors
il faut se jeter dessus!
La gloire refuse les cieux, l'amour refuse les
holocaustes mouillés. Mon Dieu, j'ai exécration
de mon orgueil!
Sans doute je ne Vous aimais pas comme il faut, mais
pour l'augmentation de ma science et de mon
plaisir.
Et je me suis trouvé devant Vous comme quelqu'un qui
s'aperçoit qu'il est seul.
Eh bien! j'ai refait connaissance avec mon néant,
j'ai regoûté à la matière dont je suis fait.
J'ai péché fortement.
Et maintenant, sauvez-moi mon Dieu, parce que c'est
assez! (Partage de Midi, Th. I, pp. 1052-1053)

[Because I have loved You
As one loves gold beautiful to look at, or a fruit;
    but then one must throw himself upon it!
Glory rejects the heavens, love rejects the sodden
    holocausts. My God, I despise my consuming
    pride!
No doubt, I did not love you as I should, but to
    augment my knowledge and my pleasure.
And I found myself confronting You like someone who
    realizes that he is alone.
So! I encountered again my nothingness, I tasted
    again the matter of which I am formed.
I have sinned greatly.
And now, save me my Lord, for this is enough!]

By then, however, (five years after Ligugé), the very thought of total renunciation is clearly obsolete. The experiment has ended in disaster and will never be attempted again. Claudel's advice seven years later to Jacques Rivière, who wanted to join the poet in China, is eloquent on that score:

Practical advice. Stay where you are and on the path traced for you. Accept the cross God gives you to bear. . . . If He did not need you where you are, He would not have put you there. Once in my life, I tried to leave my assigned post for another which I thought better, and the result was utterly catastrophic. (*Corresp.* Cl./Riv., p. 53)

Thereafter Claudel builds on the sturdy and never seriously threatened foundations of his art, inseparable from his faith.

The only fruit of Claudel's retreat at Solesmes and Ligugé is the *Ode to the Muses*.[16] In *Mémoires improvisés*, he gives the following account of its composition:

> The entire first portion [of "*Les Muses*"], 1900, was written for the most part when I was in retreat at the abbey of Solesmes, trying to find my true vocation. . . . I had seen at the Louvre a magnificent bas-relief which had made a strong impression on me. Yes, though it may be hard to believe, the poem was written in the atmosphere of Solesmes and Ligugé. (*MI*, 160)

It is hardly surprising that Claudel's perceptive Superiors at Ligugé felt that perhaps a few more years of meditation in China might not be inappropriate. The only surprising fact, in retrospect, is the magnitude of his shock upon discovering that he was not considered ready to renounce life and poetry, since "*Les Muses*" maps out, in lyrical outbursts of rare energy, the poet's future works and describes the very poetics threatened by the poet's intended renunciation.

The sarcophagus of Ostia, which he had recently seen at the Louvre, depicts on its broad face the nine Muses with their attributes; on the front side of the lid, overlooking the Muses, can be seen a bacchic feast in progress. While in retreat, Claudel is haunted by these Muses, concrete visual reminders of the poetic vocation which hangs in the balance. They so engage his imagination that they come to life, so to speak, to embody, celebrate and snatch from premature death the poetic vocation. Like a rising tide, they overrun all thoughts of renunciation; they buoy up the century's new poet, bearer of the message that must and will be carried to the four corners of the earth. Claudel's unleashed passion for his own artistic vocation is here so powerful that it makes poetic a series of statements that could be merely expository.

The sarcophagus of the Muses is clearly the pretext at hand, to use Jean Hytier's terminology;[17] it lends itself to what might be called the apparent theme, namely, the *ars poetica* unfolding in the ode. However, if we look beyond the boundaries of the poem and focus on the larger field of the whole period of Claudel's early works, we can see that the sentiment which breathes through this poem is a very complex exultation, born of despair. The explosive energy of the text issues from the triumphant rejection of renunciation, from the organic refusal on Claudel's part to let himself sink (to use his own image): "A true religious vocation" he explains in *Mémoires improvisés*, "requires that you let your boat sink; . . . it is the substitution of God's will for your own, without which it amounts to nothing" (p. 153).

Claudel's will to resist his poetic vocation had broken down, undermined by what he calls "the sly craftiness of human nature which . . . tries to protest and looks for loop-holes" (*MI,* 152), weakened by the innumerable variations his mind had played on the theme of a sacrifice too costly to be tolerable.

In *"Les Muses,"* the poet channels into the sculptured figures, viewed as embodiments of his faculties, the poetics already enunciated in *Connaissance de l'Est.* The heart of this *ars poetica* is expressed in the lines devoted to Polymnia, the Muse of religious hymns, whom Claudel singles out as the spokesman of the new poet the Creation has been waiting for:

> *Et maintenant, Polymnie, ô toi qui te tiens au milieu*
> *de tes soeurs, enveloppée dans ton long voile*
> *comme une cantatrice,*
> *Accoudée sur l'autel, accoudée sur le pupitre,*

C'est assez attendu, maintenant tu peux attaquer le
    chant nouveau! maintenant je puis entendre ta
    voix, ô mon unique! (OP, 229)

[And now, Polymnia, O you who stand in the midst of
    your sisters, enfolded in your long gown like
    a grand contralto,
Leaning on the altar, leaning on the lectern,
You have waited long enough, now you can attack the
    new song! Now I can hear your voice, O my
    only one!]

She represents the voice of the new poet-priest, the witness of
the Creation:

    . . . *tu contemples chaque chose dans ton coeur,*
        de chaque chose tu cherches comment la dire!
        (p. 230)

    [. . . you contemplate each thing in your heart,
        for each thing you seek the way to speak it!]

For the poet's special mission on earth is to make the Creation
intelligible to man, to name its objects and thereby summon
them into existence:

    Proférant de chaque chose le nom,
    Comme un père tu l'appelles mystérieusement dans
        son principe. . . . (p. 230)

    [Uttering the name of each thing,
    You invoke it mysteriously in its essential nature
        like a father.]

Claudel makes clear the irresistible secret pleasure poetic activity holds for him—a constant in his life since childhood:[18]

> *Mais je sais assez ce que veulent dire cette tête qui*
> *se tourne vers le côté, cette mine enivrée et*
> *close, et ce visage qui écoute, tout fulgurant*
> *de la jubilation orchestrale!* (p. 231)

> [But I know well the meaning of this head turned to
> one side, this drunken and withdrawn mien, this
> listening face, glowing with symphonic jubila-
> tion.]

At the peak of poetic ecstasy the poet, god-like himself, dwells among the gods, triumphantly taking them by the hand and making them join his chorus:

> *L'ode pure comme un beau corps nu tout brillant de*
> *soleil et d'huile*
> *Va chercher tous les dieux par la main pour les mêler*
> *à son choeur,*
> *Pour accueillir le triomphe à plein rire. . . .* (p. 229)

> [The pure ode, like a beautiful naked body glistening
> with sunlight and oil,
> Reaches out to take all the gods by the hand, to draw
> them into his chorus,
> To acclaim the triumph with loud laughter. . . .]

The uncontrollable poetic outburst described in the ode helps to assess not only the magnitude of the sacrifice (of his art) Claudel was contemplating, but the unlikelihood, indeed the radical impossibility, of this sacrifice:

> *Voici soudain, quand le poëte nouveau comblé de l'ex-*
> *plosion intelligible,*
> *La clameur noire de toute la vie nouée par le nombril*
> *dans la commotion de la base,*
> *S'ouvre, l'accès*

Faisant sauter la clôture, le souffle de lui-même
Violentant les mâchoires coupantes,
Le frémissant Novénaire avec un cri!
Maintenant il ne peut plus se taire! L'interrogation
    sortie de lui-même, comme du chanvre
Aux femmes de journée, il l'a confié pour toujours
Au savant choeur de l'inextinguible Echo! (p. 222)

[And now, when the new poet swollen with the intel-
    ligible explosion,
The dark clamor of all life bound at the navel in a
    fundamental stirring,
Unseals himself, the out-torrenting
Breaking through, his own profoundest breath
Assaulting his gated jaws,
The quivering Novenary with a cry,
Now he can no longer be silent! The dithyramb
    surges out of him, like hemp
To hired women, he has entrusted it forever
To the all-knowing choir of the eternally resound-
    ing Echo!]

In a rhetorical farewell, the poet rejects the literary heritage
of the Western world (symbolized by his rejection of Homer,
Virgil and Dante, *OP*, 223-225). He considers it inimical both
to his mission and to the spontaneous poetry he yearns to express,
ever ready as he is to blend with the infinitely varied voices of
the Creation:

O mon âme! le poëme n'est point fait de ces lettres
    que je plante comme des clous, mais du blanc qui
    reste sur le papier.
O mon âme! il ne faut concerter aucun plan! ô mon âme
    sauvage, il faut nous tenir libres et prêts,
Comme les immenses bandes fragiles d'hirondelles quand
    sans voix retentit l'appel automnal! (p. 224)

[O my soul! The poem is not made up of these letters
which I drive in like nails but of the white
which remains on the paper.

O my soul! One must not draw up any plan! O my savage soul, we must keep ourselves free and ready,
Like those immense flights of swallows when the
autumnal call silently resounds!]

He clings to his poetic gift with which and through which he
would explore the whole cosmos:

> *Ne quitte point mes mains, ô Lyre aux sept cordes,*
>
> . . . .
>
> *Que je voie tout entre tes fils bien tendus! et*
> *la Terre avec ses feux, et le ciel avec ses*
> *étoiles.* (p. 227)

[Do not leave my hands, O seven-stringed Lyre,

. . . .

May I see all things spread out between your
taut strings! The Earth with its fires, and
the sky with its stars.]

It seems unequivocally clear that the long-meditated plan to
become a monk has collapsed, brushed away in the sweep of the
Muses' dance.

Claudel's carefully cultivated distance from the society of man,
already evident in *Connaissance de l'Est*, is here revealed to have
arisen from the solitary pleasure he finds in contemplating the
world emptied of man,[19] in which he enters into an almost unconscious communion with the Creation:

> *Que je ne sache point ce que je dis! . . . que je*
> *sois anéanti dans mon mouvement! . . . Que*
> *je maintienne mon poids comme une lourde*
> *étoile à travers l'hymne fourmillante!* (p. 227)

[Let me know nothing of what I say! . . .
Let me be swallowed up in my own movement!
. . . May I sustain my mass like a weighty
star throughout the reverberating hymn.]

Not altogether unconscious, of course, for to contribute as poet to the universal harmony (". . . *que je sois une note en travail!*" p. 227) [. . . may I be a participating note!] he must maintain a slight pressure on his pen to record his message for humanity (*"rien que la petite pression de la main pour gouverner."* p. 227) [nothing but the slightest pressure of the hand as guide.]

The most curious thing about *"Les Muses"* is that, except for the closing invocation to Erato added in 1904, not one line bears the slightest trace of the conflict of vocations. It is as if the poet had been completely carried away by an uncontrollable outburst of poetic passion. If he could write this poem while in retreat at Solesmes and Ligugé, it would seem the best proof that his poetic vocation—with his own unconscious cooperation—had won the upper hand. Evidently Claudel did not fully realize the implications of this outburst of poetic activity. Only by assuming such unawareness can one account for the fact that at Ligugé he persisted in his plan to renounce worldly life and that he felt crushed when his offering of self was rejected.

NOTES

1 In his detailed notes on Claudel's movements in China (*Cahiers* IV, 103-116), Jean-Claude Berton mentions the poet's stay in the "infernal" port of Hankow from mid-March to early September of 1897. "At that time," writes Berton, "Hankow was known as the Chinese Chicago. It is in this hostile post . . . that Claudel begins to hear distinctly the two voices of his internal debate, to become conscious of the painful conflict in him between his desire to devote his life to God and the demands of *the profession he has chosen. Like Mesa before his rejection by God, he is trying anxiously to find his course."* (p. 107; italics are mine).

2 A letter written in Shanghai which Berton must have overlooked, since he has Claudel still travelling in Japan on June 27 (see *Cahiers* IV, p. 109).

3 *Paul Claudel, Francis Jammes, Gabriel Frizeau: Correspondance (1897-1938)* (Paris: Gallimard, 1952), p. 26.

4 "It seems to me that careful consideration of this matter leads to two possible conclusions: either the writer speaks to the people . . . to amuse or instruct . . . or he speaks *instead of the people*, by virtue of that tacit delegation consented to by the public, who stops talking and begins to listen as soon as the actor opens his mouth.

While on stage or off, the actor relieves, he "purges" the people's heart of their unformulated and obscure life [*il soulage, il "purge" la multitude du souffle informulé qu'elle portait dans son sein confus*]. That is how the Greeks conceived of the theater, predicated entirely on the protagonist emerging from the anonymous chorus to speak and then returning to it [*Là était plutôt l'idée du théâtre antique que constitue tout seul un protagoniste sortant du choeur anonyme et y rentrant*]. (*Cahiers* I, 107; the italics are Claudel's)

5 Francis Jammes, *Oeuvres* (Paris: Mercure de France, 1921) , II, 25. *Quatorze prières* was published in 1898 at Orthez in a private edition.

6 *Paul Claudel et André Gide: Correspondance (1899-1926)* (Paris: Gallimard, 1949), p. 45. Gide is delighted with Claudel's qualified praise of his talent. On December 13, 1907, he writes in his *Journal*: "I have just reread a forgotten letter from P. Claudel (1899): 'Your mind has not a single slant,' he told me. Exactly what is needed. No praise can be better for me" (*André Gide, Journal, 1889-1939*, Bibliothèque de la Pléiade (Paris: Gallimard, 1939) , p. 257) .

7 See Chaigne, *Vie*, p. 78.

8 Paul Claudel, *OP*, 206-217. This essay was first published in the May 1903 issue of the *Mercure de France* and appended to the 1907 edition of *Art Poétique*. A short lyrical history of church architecture, it is in the style and tone of *Connaissance de l'Est*.

9 For Jammes's account of that meeting, see Francis Jammes, *Les Caprices du poète (Mémoires)* (Paris: Plon, 1923), III, 86-96.

10 This ambiguous phrase has both a social and a theological meaning: it can be rendered: "one moves in society" or "one lives in the world"—as opposed to monastic life.

11 The play was published in the June, July and August 1900 issues of *L'Ermitage*.

12 This letter is missing from the volume of the *Corresp.* Cl./Jam./Friz.

13 Chaigne quotes François Guédon's article, which had appeared in *Semaine religieuse de Paris*, April 23, 1960 (*Vie*, p. 82, n.58).

14 Berton, without giving his sources, extends this stay to two months (October and November) in his recent biographical notes on Claudel in *Cahiers* PC, IV, p. 111.

15 The small "*s*" in "*supérieurs*," which must be a misprint, normally refers to lay superiors who, in this case, ironically enough, would be officials of the Ministry of Foreign Affairs.

16 Paul Claudel, "*Les Muses*," *OP*, 221-233.

17 See Jean Hytier, *Les Arts de littérature*, Editions Charlot (Paris, 1945) , p. 17.

18 Cf. Guillemin, "*Claudel avant sa 'conversion*,'" *RP*, May 1955, p. 94.

19 Cf. Claudel's letter to Frizeau of August 1, 1905: ". . . how beautiful are the Pyrenees and how good it feels on these heights where man is no longer present!" (*Corresp.* Cl./Jam./Friz., p. 52).

CHAPTER VI

In Quest of Love:
From Reality to Vision

The outburst of *"Les Muses"* foreshadows a passionate explosion of a different order. Shortly after his disastrous retreat at Ligugé, Claudel sails for China (mid-October 1900).[1] On the boat he falls in love with a married woman and involves himself in a relationship that lasts four years. This episode is transposed in *Partage de Midi*, composed in the winter of 1905.

From 1901 to 1903, Claudel writes relatively little ("For two years," he told André Gide in 1905, "I stopped writing. I thought I should sacrifice art to religion").[2] However, he did write at least four of the nine poems added to *Connaissance de l'Est* (1900-1905)[3]—*"Le Riz," "Le Point," "Libation au jour futur,"* and *"Le Jour de la fête de tous-les-fleuves"*—published in the November 1903 issue of *L'Occident*.[4] In 1903 he begins the composition of *Art Poétique*, completed in 1904. Also in 1904 he writes the invocation to Erato which completes *"Les Muses,"* left unfinished since 1900.[5]

In *Art Poétique* Claudel presents certain metaphysical arguments, already implicit in some of the prose poems of *Connaissance de l'Est* in support of his concept of the Universe. His basic postulates, analyzed extensively by Pierre Angers in his *Commentaire à l'Art Poétique*,[6] are that in the Universe each order of the Creation alludes to all the others and finds its *raison d'être* only in its relationship to the whole, and that the whole is homogeneous and continuous in Time.

In Claudel's Universe, man not only occupies a precise position but also is endowed with a specific vocation: his intelligence and his freedom permit him to discover the meaning of the great drama of which he is a part and, in fact, to direct it towards its goal. For man is a special delegate on earth. He has been granted the power to speak, the credentials to interpret the Creation and the mission to re-offer it in homage to God. His ambivalent position on earth makes him the mediator of the Creation, for, on the one hand, he partakes of the creativity of God and, on the other, he is himself created and "solidary" to the Universe. Thus he is a vital link between God and the Creation.

As creature, his rôle consists in submitting to the order established by the Master. His specific vocation is to assume the duties of his condition as creature, along with its contingent sacrifices. For man, as Claudel has explained in a letter to Jacques Rivière, is made for God, whether or not he derives from this condition good or ill, although to be sure, Claudel hastens to add, "only good can come of it" (*Corresp.* Cl./Riv., p. 256).

The relationship of man to God and of man to the Universe expresses the immutable order of things. It cannot be abolished. Being endowed with free will, man can of course elect to turn his back on his own vocation. This would, however, constitute a misuse of his freedom, which has been granted him for the sole purpose of his freely choosing his assigned destiny. In his contacts with the Universe, writes Angers, elucidating Claudel's thought, man discovers the demands which God makes upon him. If he is reluctant to respond to them he ought only to blame the moral wretchedness resulting from his sins (*Commentaire*, p. 47).

Claudel's unsystematic presentation in *Art Poétique*, his impatience with carefully sustained arguments and his sudden lyrical outbursts inevitably raise the question of the philosophical merit of this work. Angers feels that it has great merit as philosophy. He does, however, acknowledge serious defects: the lack of precision in the exposition of complex problems; the diffuse style, which sacrifices clarity to preserve the freshness of experience; difficulties on Claudel's part in handling the abstractions of logic, and inability to translate accurately subtle philosophical concepts which the poet "feels" rather than understands (p. 49).

What Claudel attempts in *Art Poétique* is to construct an ideological base to support his chosen mission. He is convinced that he has now understood the true meaning of God's injunction. This is confirmed by his answer to a survey conducted in 1905 by Georges Le Cardonnel and Charles Vellay in which leading poets were asked to consider the following question: "What in your opinion is the dominant tendency of contemporary poetry? What do you foresee will be the poetry of tomorrow?" Claudel answered as follows: "[The poet] has a general rather than a special utility. He is more like a clock than a baker. As thinker, his responsibility is to think, and as writer, to write, for the public, for the people: *for* meaning here *instead of*" (italics are Claudel's).[7] In short, the Creation is in need of verbalization and it is the poet's mission to speak for inarticulate man.

In 1900 Claudel had left the ode to the Muses unfinished. The completed portion already contained the outline of his poetic program, ending with the boast that he was ready to implement it, presumably in a large work encompassing the whole Creation:

> *J'ai trouvé le secret; je sais parler; si je veux,*
> *je saurai vous dire*
> *Cela que chaque chose veut dire.*
> *Je suis initié au silence; il y a l'inexhaustible*
> *cérémonie vivante, il y a un monde à envahir,*
> *il y a un poème insatiable à remplir par la*
> *production des céréales et de tous les fruits.*
> (OP, 231; italics are Claudel's)

> [I have discovered the secret: I know how to speak;
>   if I wish I could tell you
> What each thing *means and yearns to say.*
> I am an adept of silence; there is the inexhaustible

living rite, there is a world to invade, there
is an insatiable poem to be filled with the
harvest of grain and fruits.]

The poem breaks off at this point, with one more line to indicate
the break and to hint at a setback, but without any reference to
the disaster of Ligugé:

> —*Je laisse cette tâche à la terre; je refuis vers
> l'Espace ouvert et vide* (p. 231).

> [I leave this task to the earth; once again I flee
> towards the open and empty spaces.]

The *"espace ouvert et vide"* is the sea—the poet is sailing back
to China (October, 1900).

If Claudel did not finish *"Les Muses"* before 1904, it is in part
because he did not know how to finish it, as André Gide, quoting
Claudel, has recorded in his *Journal* (December 5, 1905).[8] He
eventually found an ending that satisfied him by identifying
Erato, the Muse of erotic poetry, with Ysé of *Partage de Midi*.
It is Erato who, in the ode, threatens to interfere with the imple-
mentation of the poetic program as the religious vocation had
done at Ligugé.[9] The difference is that Erato succeeds. We are
dealing here with a double symbol which remains obscure in the
ode, but becomes clear in the play, composed the following year.
Erato in *"Les Muses"* appears as a Dionysian figure:

> . . . *et moi je suis chaude et folle, impatiente et nue!*
> *Que fais-tu ici encore? Baise-moi et viens!*
> *Brise, arrache tous les liens! prends-moi ta déesse*
>   *avec toi!* (p. 232)

> [. . . as for me, I am hot and wild, impatient and
>   naked!
> What are you still doing here! Kiss me and come with me!

Break, tear off all bonds! Take me, your goddess, with
  you.]

Her words evoke the Dionysian factor in poetic inspiration. As
the Muse representing poetic ecstasy, she refuses to serve a poetic
objective which prudently caters simultaneously to the requirements of the poet's two vocations:

> Combien de temps vas-tu t'occuper encore, bien
>   régulièrement, entre mes sages soeurs,
> Comme un maître au milieu de son équipe d'ouvrières?
>   (p. 232)

[How long are you going to concern yourself, in such
  an orderly way, with my wise sisters,
Like an overseer among his team of workwomen!]

At the same time, Erato serves another function:

> Ne comprends-tu point mon ennui, et que mon désir est
>   de toi-même? ce fruit à dévorer entre nous deux,
>   ce grand feu à faire de nos deux âmes! (p. 232)

[Don't you understand my weariness, and that my desire
  is for you! This fruit to be devoured by the two
  of us, this great fire to be made of our two
  souls!]

She is destined to play in the poet's life a rôle which the ode does
not really clarify:

> Erato! tu me regardes, et je lis une résolution dans
>   tes yeux!
> Je lis une réponse, je lis une question dans tes yeux!
>   Une réponse et une question dans tes yeux!
> Le hourra qui prend en toi de toutes parts comme de
>   l'or, comme du feu dans le fourrage!

Une réponse dans tes yeux! Une réponse et une question
dans tes yeux. (p. 233)

[Erato! You look at me, and I read a resolve in your
   eyes!
I read a reply, I read a question in your eyes! A reply
   and a question in your eyes!
The hurrah which flames up in every part of you, like
   gold, like a fire in the grasslands!
A reply in your eyes! A reply and a question in your
   eyes!]

It is in *Partage de Midi*, where Erato becomes Ysé, that the Muse
realizes her full potentialities.

If Claudel's conversion of 1886 spiritualized the love-quest of
L'Endormie, opening the door to renunciation, *Partage de
Midi*[10] dramatizes a regression to the love-quest after the failure
of his attempt at total renunciation. After the long drawn-out
battle between poetic and religious vocations, the old problems
of the love-quest are renewed and relived with an intensity and
urgency born of personal experience. Claudel's obsession with
renunciation brought to a crisis by the conflict between the
poet's two vocations is now recast and humanized by a great passion. It assumes the form of a conception of love centered on renunciation, on freely accepted separation, in the very name of
love.[11]

In his 1948 preface to the first public edition of *Partage de
Midi* (*Th.* I, 983) Claudel shows quite obviously that he has cast
himself in his own play, or, to be more precise, he has dramatized
the crisis of Ligugé and the encounter on the boat. His purpose
in writing the play is to assess the significance not only of these
events, but indeed of all the past years, from the time of his first
"illumination" at Notre-Dame in 1886. By the time he writes
Partage (in September-November of 1905), he has already gained
sufficient detachment to place the more recent events in the
broader perspective of the last twenty years of trial and to view

them in the light of his deepening knowledge of Christian doctrine. He knows, for instance, from his reading of Saint Augustine, that in the life of him who is chosen, everything can be beneficial, even his sins (*MI*, 181), that good and evil are mysteriously connected in the scheme of divine Providence. Already in *Repos* (1896) he had used a striking image to suggest the beneficial effect of evil ("Evil in the world is like a slave who labors to bring up water . . ." *Th.* I, 848). In *Partage*, Mesa's adulterous love affair with Ysé, his responsibility in the death of her husband and Ysé's murder of her illegitimate child are sins and crimes illustrating the ways of Providence, "which utilizes every means to achieve its ends" (*MI*, 181).

In the first act of the play the lovers "recognize" each other ("Mesa, I am Ysé, it is I," p. 1003). They are predestined souls; their fall is foreseen by Providence. "Did you have the feeling at the time," Amrouche asked Claudel, "that the encounter on the boat had a character of necessity in relation to yourself, to your destiny?" "I had the overwhelming feeling," explained Claudel, "that it could not be otherwise . . . that I was caught in a kind of trap from which there was no escaping" (*MI*, 182). In *Partage*, what these predestined complementary souls discover in each other is not the possibility of human fulfillment, but rather the radical impossibility of fulfillment: "I am the impossible" explains Ysé (p. 1004). In that sense, their indispensability is providential, and Claudel thinks it reasonable to assume that complementary souls "exist for no other purpose than to serve as key to each other . . ." (*OC*, XI, 306). It is their agonizing non-fulfillment here on earth that drives them towards realization of the most perfect spiritual union. Claudel has here subverted the old concept of complementary souls, proposed in jest by Aristophanes in Plato's *Symposium*, with happiness replaced by suffering as the handmaiden of divine Providence. The passion of Mesa and Ysé condemns them to death. Their ultimate vision, the very condition of their love, is the dissolution of their earthly beings in order to achieve a spiritual union beyond death:

Mais ce que nous désirons, ce n'est point de créer,
mais de détruire, et que ah!
Il n'y ait plus rien d'autre que toi et moi, et en
toi que moi, et en moi que ta possession, et la
rage, et la tendresse, et de te détruire et de
n'être plus gênée
Détestablement par ces vêtements de chair, et ces
cruelles dents dans mon coeur,
Non point cruelles!
Ah, ce n'est point le bonheur que je t'apporte, mais
ta mort, et la mienne avec elle,
Mais qu'est-ce que cela me fait à moi que je te fasse
mourir,
Et moi, et tout, et tant pis! pourvu qu'à ce prix
qui est toi et moi,
Donnés, jetés, arrachés, lacérés, consumés,
Je sente ton âme, un moment qui est toute l'éternité,
toucher,
Prendre
La mienne comme la chaux astreint le sable en brûlant
et en sifflant! (Th. I, 1030)

[But what we desire is not to create but to destroy,
and that
There be nothing else but you and I, and in you only
me, and in me only the possession of you, and
rage and tenderness, and to destroy you and to
be no longer detestably
Restrained by this fleshly apparel, and those cruel
teeth in my heart,
Not cruel!
Oh, I do not bring you happiness, but your death, and
mine with it.
But what does it matter to me that I should cause you
to die,
And myself, and everything, too bad! So long as, at this price,
which is you and I

Surrendered, thrown down, torn, lacerated, consumed I
    feel your soul, for a moment which is all eternity,
    touch
Take
Mine as lime seizes the sand, burning and hissing.]

Mesa's reply, in this scene, clearly associates Ysé of *Partage*
with Erato of *"Les Muses"*:

Ne me sois plus étrangère!
Je le lis enfin, et j'en ai horreur, dans tes yeux
    le grand appel panique!
Derrière tes yeux qui me regardent la grande flamme
    noire de l'âme qui brûle de toutes parts comme
    une cité dévorée! (pp. 1030-1031)

[Do not be a stranger to me any longer!
At last I read in your eyes the great panic summons,
    and I am horrified by it!
Behind your eyes which gaze at me the great dark
    flame of the soul which burns everywhere,
    like a razed city!]

This *"grand appel panique,"* which he sees in her eyes, is reminiscent of, yet presents a strong contrast with, what the poet sees
in Erato's eyes:

Le hourra qui prend en toi de toutes parts comme de
    l'or, comme du feu dans le fourrage! (OP, 233)

[The hurrah which flares up in every part of you like
    gold, like fire in the grasslands!]

There is implied here an idea Claudel develops later in the
fourth ode, *"La Muse qui est la Grâce,"* namely that poetic
ecstasy is related to, but at the same time incompatible with,
mystical ecstasy—both represented by the same Muse. The fourth

ode dramatizes this relationship, as its prefatory *"Argument"*
explains:

> *Invasion de l'ivresse poétique. Dialogue du poète avec la
> Muse qui devient peu à peu la Grâce. Il essaye de la refouler,
> il lui demande de le laisser à son devoir humain, à la place
> de son âme il lui offre l'univers entier qu'il va recréer par
> l'intelligence et la parole. En vain, c'est à lui personnelle-
> ment que la Muse qui est la Grâce ne cesse de s'adresser!
> C'est la joie divine qu'elle lui rappelle et son devoir de
> sanctification personnelle.* (p. 263).

[Insurgence of the poetic drunkenness. Dialogue of the poet
with the Muse who little by little becomes Grace. He tries
to force her back, he asks her to leave him to his human
duty, instead of his soul he offers her the entire universe
which he will recreate by his intelligence and by the word.
In vain, it is to him personally that the Muse who is Grace
unceasingly addresses herself! It is divine joy that she reminds him of, and his duty of personal sanctification.]

In the fourth ode, the poet resists this solicitation in a vigorous
rejection of renunciation:

> —*Va-t'en! Je me retourne désespérement vers la*
>   *terre!*
> *Va-t'en! tu ne m'ôteras point ce froid goût de la*
>   *terre,*
> *Cette obstination avec la terre qu'il y a dans la*
>   *moelle de mes os et dans le caillou*
>   *de ma substance et dans le*
>   *noir noyau de mes viscères!*
> *Vainement! tu ne me consumeras point!*
> *Vainement! plus tu m'appelles avec cette présence de*
>   *feu et plus je retire en bas vers le sol solide,*
> *Comme un grand arbre qui s'en va rechercher le roc et*
>   *le tuf de l'embrassement et de la vis de ses*
>   *quatre-vingt-deux racines!* (p. 276)

[Go away! I despairingly turn toward the earth!
Go away! You will not take from me this cold taste
     for the earth,
This obsession with the earth which is in the mar-
     row of my bones and in the rock of my substance,
     and in the dark pit of my bowels!
In vain! You will not consume me!
In vain! The more you call to me with this presence
     of fire, the more I pull back towards solid
     ground,
Like the huge tree which seeks out the boulder and
     bedrock with the twisting embrace of its
     eighty-two roots!]

By connecting his own disappointment at Ligugé with the
encounter of Ysé in a providential relationship, Claudel invites
a comparison between God's rejection of Mesa and Ysé's rejection of her lover, the latter occurring between the second and
third acts of the play. After the adultery is consummated in the
second act Ysé replaces God in Mesa's heart:

> Ysé: *Sais-tu bien ce que tu fais, Mesa?*
> Mesa: *Je ne sais que toi, Ysé.*
> Ysé: *D'un côté Ysé, et de cet autre,*
>   *Tout moins que je n'y suis pas.*
> Mesa: *Je te préfère, Ysé!* (*Th.* I, 1029)

> [*Ysé:* Do you fully understand what you are doing,
>   Mesa?
> *Mesa:* I know only you, Ysé.
> *Ysé:* On one side Ysé, and on the other, every-
>   thing but me.
> *Mesa:* It is you I prefer, Ysé!]

This reflects accurately God's relationship to the world in Claudel's theology: "There is only one God, there is only one essential
way of differing from God, since all things have this in common,

that they are not God" (*Corresp.* Cl./Riv., p. 48). Ysé now stands at one side and the rest of the world at the other. God seems to have disappeared.

In the first act, Mesa had made a profound observation about human love: ". . . all love is but comedy/ Between man and woman; the real questions are not posed" (*Th.* I, 1000). These words now assume their prophetic meaning, for the transfer of Mesa's love from God to Ysé is a comedy for which Ysé will not forgive Mesa. She leaves him to follow Amalric.

The reasons for Ysé's desertion are gradually brought to light in the third act. She tells her new lover, Amalric, that her presence was hurting Mesa and that she actually sacrificed herself for his sake. In fact, both secretly wished to separate: "It is true, I intensely desired that you go," Mesa admits later; and she, in turn, yearned for a way out of this "love which is death" (pp. 1044-1045).

> *Un an.*
> *Un an cela dura ainsi et je sentais qu'il était captif,*
> *Mais que je ne le possédais pas, et quelque chose en*
>   *lui d'étranger*
> *Impossible.*
> *Qu'a-t-il donc à me reprocher? parce qu'il ne s'est*
>   *pas donné, et moi, je me suis retirée.* (p. 1043)

> [One year.
> One year it lasted thus and I felt that he was caught,
> Except that I did not possess him and something in
>   him impossibly
> Alien.
> Why then should he reproach me? For he did not
>   give himself, and for my part, I withdrew.]

When Mesa finds her again, his first impulse is to put the blame on her:

Ce grand trésor que je porte en moi,
Tu n'as point pu le déraciner,
Le prendre. . . .

[This great treasure which I carry within me,
You have not been able to uproot it,
To take it. . . .]

But then he admits:

. . . je n'ai pas su le donner. . . . Il fallait
*   tout donner,*
Et c'est cela que tu n'as pas pardonné. (p. 1047)

[. . . I did not know how to give it. . . . I
should have given everything,
And that is what you have not forgiven.]

Thus is re-enacted, but this time in the shape of an earthly passion, the crisis which resulted in Claudel's rejection at Ligugé, and the idol has proven as uncompromising as the Master. In the third act Ysé abandons Mesa once more. This time she abandons him, helpless and wounded, in a house that is mined and about to explode. She is fleeing from civil war and choosing life with Amalric, rather than certain death with Mesa. However, she reappears in order to share Mesa's fate.

The first two acts, largely biographical, dramatize Claudel's own love affair: "I was thirty-two years old at the time," writes Claudel to Massignon in 1908, "the truly critical age, and the first two acts of *Partage de Midi* contain nothing but an accurate account of the horrible adventure in which I nearly lost my soul and my life, after ten years of Christian life and absolute chastity" (Chaigne, *Vie*, p. 84). The third act, by far the most important to Claudel,[12] transforms Ysé—the embodiment of human love—into an instrument of Providence. Mesa's christianization is brought about by the intervention of love. Cleansed of all conceit, he achieves humility:[13]

Non, non, mon Dieu! Allez, je ne Vous demande rien!

. . . .

Mon Dieu, j'ai exécration de mon orgueil! (*Th.* I, 1052)

[No, no, my God! No, I ask nothing of You!

. . . .

My God, I despise my consuming pride!]

In the closing scene of the play, death and transfiguration are preceded by the spiritual marriage of Mesa and Ysé (pp. 1059-1060). This scene was written a month before Claudel's engagement on December 28, 1905, and three months before his marriage in March 1906.

In the fifth ode, "*La Maison fermée,*" Claudel will praise marriage as a form of self-submission to Law. The poet's wife, in that ode, becomes his guiding angel who will remind him of his commitment:

—*Et la gardienne du poëte répond: Dieu m'a posée sa gardienne,*
Afin qu'il rende à chacun ce qui lui est dû,
L'homme à l'homme, à la femme ce qu'il tient de la femme,
Et à Dieu seul ce qu'il a reçu de Dieu seul, qui est un esprit de prière et de parole. (*OP,* 279)

[*And the guardian of the poet replies:* God has made me his guardian,
So that he can give everyone his due,
Man to man, to woman what he has in him of woman,
And to God alone what he has received from God alone, which is a gift of prayer and speech.]

Addressing her husband, she declares:

La poutre de notre maison n'est pas de cèdre, les boiseries de notre chambre ne sont pas de cyprès,

*Mais goûte l'ombre, mon mari, de la demeure bénite
  entre ces murs épais qui nous protègent de
  l'air extérieur et du froid.*

. . . .

*L'âge vient, tu as assez longtemps erré, démeurons
  ensemble avec la Sagesse.
Comment ferait-elle ménage avec les vieux garçons,
  chez qui il n'y a rien qui ferme?
Leur coeur est tourné au dehors, mais le nôtre est
  tourné au dedans vers Dieu . . . (p. 279)*

[The beams of our house are not cedar, the wood-
  work of our bedroom is not cypress,
But taste the shade, my husband, of this blessed
  home between these thick walls which protect
  us from the outside air and from the cold.

. . . .

Age comes, you have wandered long enough, let us
  live together, with Wisdom.
How could she live among old bachelors, in whom there
  is nothing which closes?
Their hearts are turned outwards, but ours is turned
  inwards to God. . . .]

She even adds a word of warning:

*Tu as donné ta parole. Garde-la pour qu'elle te
  garde et ne va pas en faire commerce comme
  du vieux vêtement que l'on vend au Chananéen.*
  (p. 280)

[You have given your word. Keep it that it may
  keep you, and do not barter with it like
  an old coat one sells to a Canaanite.]

This was written in 1908, two years after Claudel's own marriage. It represents the "official" terminal point of the crisis of
Partage (which will, however, continue to occupy the poet's

thoughts to the end of his life). "*La Maison fermée,*" the new-founded home, closes the door on destructive self-indulgence (cf. *L'Echange*) and symbolizes God's finite but inexhaustible world which, for Claudel, is the only valid object of poetic exploration:

> *O certitude et immensité de mon domaine! ô cher*
> *univers entre mes mains connaissantes! ô*
> *considération du nombre parfait à qui rien*
> *ne peut être soustrait ou ajouté!*
> *O Dieu, rien n'existe que par une image de votre*
> *perfection!*
> *Est-ce qu'aucune de vos créatures peut vous échapper?*
> *mais vous les tenez captives par des règles*
> *aussi sévères que celle d'un coeur pénitent et*
> *avec une loi ascétique.*
> *Et vous qui connaissez le nombre de nos cheveux, est-*
> *ce que vous ignorez celui de vos étoiles? (OP. 281)*

> [O certitude and immensity of my domain! O dear
> universe in my knowing hands! O considera-
> tion of the perfect number to which nothing
> can be added or subtracted!
> O God, nothing exists except through an image of
> your perfection!
> Can a single one of your creatures escape from
> you? But you hold them captive by rules as
> severe as that of a penitent heart and with
> an ascetic law.
> And you who know every hair on our heads, would
> you not know the number of the stars?]

Claudel reaches here a position diametrically opposed to Rimbaud's, whose visionary explorations into the limitless unknown he has now safely rejected: "The idea of a world finite and closed . . . is for me a source of light," he writes to Rivière on January 28, 1908 (*Corresp.* Cl./Riv., p. 129). His period of exploration is essentially over. He is forty years old and there will be no more major crises in his life. To be sure, much remains to be subdued in this pagan spirit turned Christian. "Do not think," he once told Rivière, "that one can become a true Christian and not accept a degree of stultification and even mutilation" (p. 68). As Claudel's yearning for sainthood increased in intensity, poetry came to the rescue as an instrument of self-preservation and the poetics came into focus as it became an antidote to "self-mutilation."

Claudel's early works are the battleground of this struggle for survival; the dynamics of his conflict account for the genesis of these works. The character of the conflict itself evolves considerably in the course of these first twenty years: originally a diffuse love-quest (as in *L'Endormie*) invited, by a mystical experience, to transcend itself, it becomes a dramatic clash between a manifest artistic destiny and the lure of sainthood. The conciliation of these tendencies is at the heart of Claudel's poetics.

NOTES

1 The exact departure date is probably October 19, 1900. Claudel's last letter from Paris to Pottecher, dated Friday, October 12, announces: "I am leaving next Friday for Foochow" (*Cahiers PC* I, 108). In his notes on Claudel's movements, Jean-Claude Berton has apparently confused departure and arrival (cf. *Cahiers PC* IV, 111).

2 André Gide, *Journal (1889-1939)*, p. 190. Claudel, eager to convert his friend to Catholicism, evidently did not mention his love-affair—the major cause of his relative unproductiveness during this period. Had he done so, it seems safe to assume that Gide would have recorded it in this same journal entry of December 5, 1905, which gives a detailed account of his recent conversation with Claudel.

3 Paul Claudel, *OP*, pp. 108-120.

4 These dates of 1900-1905 are composition dates. Three of the poems, "*La Lampe et la cloche*," "*La Délivrance d'Amaterasu*," and "*Visite*" (*OP*, pp. 108-115), were not published until 1907, in the second Mercure de France edition (augmented) of *Connaissance de l'Est*. They precede, without editorial explanation, the other six poems which were published earlier, in *L'Occident* (November 1903; May 1905). This order is followed in all subsequent editions, down to *OP* (1957) and the 1960 Mercure de France reissue of this text. The last poem, "*Dissolution*," was written at sea in February or March, 1905 and was published in May of that same year in *L'Occident*—soon after Claudel's return to France. It contains the first reference to his recent love affair ("*ce visage beaucoup aimé* [her beloved face]" *OP.*, p. 120, published, curiously enough, a year before the private edition of *Partage de Midi*.

5 In his introduction to the Pléiade edition of Claudel's *Oeuvre poétique* (1957), Stanislas Fumet notes: " '*Les Muses*' was composed in Paris in 1900, before Claudel's return to China. The concluding portion only was added by the poet in 1901 in Foochow. The date of 1904, at the end of the poem, indicates the time Claudel tran-

scribed the poem for the printer" (p. xviii). This new dating is based on *Mémoires improvisés* (p. 160). Fumet simply follows this source without other supporting evidence for this very important change in the traditional dating of that portion of the text. Jacques Madaule maintains the older dating in his introduction to the 1956 edition of *Théâtre* (*Th.* I, p. xxxvi). André Gide's journal entry of December 5, 1905 confirms the older dating (see note 8 below).

6 Pierre Angers, *Commentaire à l'Art Poétique de Paul Claudel, avec le texte de l'Art Poétique* (Paris: Mercure de France, 1949). All our references to *Art Poétique* are to the text in this edition.

7 Georges Le Cardonnel and Charles Vellay, eds., *La Littérature contemporaine (1905): opinions des écrivains de ce temps* (Paris: Mercure de France, 1905), pp. 170-171. Claudel's reply has been reprinted in *OC*, XVIII, 11.

8 "*The Ode to the Muses,* [Claudel] told us, begun in 1900, remained for a long time unfinished. He did not know 'how to finish it.' It was only in 1904 that he added the invocation to Erato and the end" (p. 190).

9 Cf. Chaigne (*Vie,* p. 82) who quotes, as a sample of the Solesmes literary production, lines taken from the invocation to Erato written later, in China. He even pinpoints the moment of dramatic renunciation in a graphic conclusion drawn from these lines taken quite literally: "And it is probably then, after Claudel had just written, '*Et en effet je sentis, je sentis sa main sur ma main* [Yes I felt, I felt her hand on mine]' that he drops his pen or breaks it, determined never to write again" (p. 82). See the two recent reviews of Chaigne's *Vie de Paul Claudel* in *Bulletin de la société Paul Claudel,* No. 7, May 1961, pp. 14-16 (Pierre Moreau), and *Cahiers Paul Claudel, IV,* pp. 357-361 (Jean Noël Segrestaa). His numerous "*inédits*" for which we are all thankful, do not compensate for a growing list of errors.

10 Paul Claudel, *Th.* 987-1064.

11 "*Ce que c'est que d'être séparé de son amour il n'était pas trop tôt que je l'apprisse de toutes les manières*" ("*Ode jubilaire,*" *OP,* 673) [The time had come for me to learn, in all its forms, what it is to be separated from one's love.]

12 Cf. Claudel's letter of September 19, 1905, to Francis Jammes: "It is not the passions that I wish to paint, but the *passion* of an unfortunate soul" (*Corresp.* Cl./Jam./Friz., p. 62).

13 Cf. Claudel's description of Mesa, written a few days before the first performance of *Partage* on December 17, 1948:

Mesa, le héros de *Partage, est . . . un pharisien sous sa forme la plus mesquine, un "sacré petit bourgeois," comme le lui dira cruellement Ysé. Un avare, un égoïste, un sucré, un rétreci, un dur, un confit, uniquement préoccupé de lui-même, parfaitement insoucieux et incurieux du prochain. L'aventure du chemin de Damas qui s'est renouvelée bizarrement à son profit ne l'a pas essentiellement transformé. Elle a simplement accentué en lui le sentiment de la différence et de la supériorité. . . ." (*OC,* XI, 305)*

[Mesa, the hero of *Partage,* is . . . a pharisee of the meanest kind, a "dirty *petit bourgeois,*" as Ysé will cruelly tell him. Miserly, selfish, sugary, narrow-minded, pig-headed, sanctimonious, exclusively preoccupied with himself, completely heedless and oblivious of others. The encounter on the road to Damascus which strangely reoccurred for his benefit did not essentially transform him. It simply accentuated in him his feeling of being different and superior. . . .]

SELECTED BIBLIOGRAPHY

I. Editions of Claudel's Works Used in this Study.

Claudel, Paul. *Oeuvres complètes.* In process of publication. Paris: Gallimard, 1950- .

──────. *Oeuvre poétique.* Introduction par Stanislas Fumet. Bibliothèque de la Pléiade. Paris: Gallimard, 1957.

──────. *Théâtre.* Introduction et chronologie de la vie et de l'oeuvre par Jacques Madaule. 2 vols. Bibliothèque de la Pléiade. Paris: Gallimard, 1954.

Paul Claudel: *Mémoires improvisés.* Recueillis par Jean Amrouche. 4th ed. Paris: Gallimard, 1954.

Paul Claudel et André Gide: Correspondance (1899-1926). Préface et notes par Robert Mallet. 5th ed. Paris: Gallimard, 1949.

Paul Claudel, Francis Jammes, Gabriel Frizeau: Correspondance (1897-1938), avec des lettres de Jacques Rivière. Préface et notes par André Blanchet. 2nd ed. Paris: Gallimard, 1952.

Jacques Rivière et Paul Claudel: Correspondance (1907-1914). Introduction par Isabelle Rivière. Paris: Plon, 1926.

André Suarès et Paul Claudel: Correspondance (1904-1938). Préface et notes par Robert Mallet. Paris: Gallimard, 1951.

II. Critical Works.

Angers, Pierre. *Commentaire à l'Art Poétique de Paul Claudel, avec le texte de l'Art Poétique.* Paris: Mercure de France, 1949.

Antoine, Gérald. *Les Cinq Grandes Odes de Claudel, ou la poésie de la répétition.* Paris: Lettres Modernes, 1959.

Augst, Bertrand. "L'Otage de Paul Claudel," *The Romanic Review,* LIII (February 1962), 32-51.

Barjon, Louis. *Paul Claudel. Préface de Paul Claudel.* Paris: Editions Universitaires, 1953.

Beaumont, Ernest. *Le Sens de l'amour dans le théâtre de Claudel: le thème de Beatrice.* Paris: Lettres Modernes, 1958.

Bonnefoy, Yves. *Rimbaud par lui-même.* Paris: Editions du Seuil, 1961.

Bremond, Henri. *Prière et poésie.* Paris: Grasset, 1926.

Cahiers Paul Claudel. Vol. I: *"Tête d'Or" et les débuts littéraires.* 5th ed. Paris: Gallimard, 1959. Vol. II. *Le Rire de Paul Claudel.* 1960.

Chaigne, Louis. *Vie de Paul Claudel et genèse de son oeuvre.* Tours: Mame, 1961.

Clouard, Henri. *Histoire de la littérature française, du symbolisme à nos jours.* Vol. I: *De 1885 à 1914.* Paris: Albin Michel, 1960.

Etiemble. *Le Mythe de Rimbaud.* Vol. II. 3rd ed. Paris: Gallimard, 1952.

Fowlie, Wallace. *Paul Claudel.* New York: Hillary House, 1957.

Gide, André. *Journal: 1889-1939.* Bibliothèque de la Pléiade. Paris: Gallimard, 1939.

———. *Oeuvres complètes d'André Gide.* Vol. II. Edition augmentée de textes inédits, établie par L. Martin-Chauffier. Paris: Gallimard, 1933.

Grossvogel, David I. *20th Century French Drama.* New York: Columbia University Press, Paperback Edition, 1961, pp. 107-123.

Guicharnaud, Jacques with June Beckelman. *Modern French Theatre from Giraudoux to Beckett.* New Haven: Yale University Press Paperbound, 1961, pp. 69-89.

Guillemin, Henri. *Claudel et son art d'écrire.* 8th ed. Paris: Gallimard, 1955.

Guillemin, Henri. "Claudel jusqu'à sa 'conversion,' " *La Revue de Paris* (April 1955), 20-30.

———. "Claudel avant sa 'conversion,' " *La Revue de Paris* (May 1955), 89-100.

———. *Zola, légende ou vérité?* Paris: Julliard, 1960.

Hubert, Renée Riese. "Claudel, poète en prose," *The French Review,* XXXV (February 1962), 369-376.

Hytier, Jean. *Les Arts de littérature.* Paris: Charlot, 1945.

Le Cardonnel, Georges and Charles Vellay. *La Littérature contemporaine (1905): opinions des écrivains de ce temps.* Paris: Mercure de France, 1905, pp. 170-171.

Lefèvre, Frédéric. *Les Sources de Paul Claudel.* Paris: Lemercier, 1927.

Madaule, Jacques. *Le Génie de Paul Claudel.* 2nd ed. Paris: Desclée de Brouwer, 1933.

Madaule, Jacques. *Le Drame de Paul Claudel.* Préface de Paul Claudel. Paris: Desclée de Brouwer, 1936.

———. *Paul Claudel, dramaturge.* Paris: L'Arche, 1956.

Mauvrocordato, Alexandre. *L'Ode de Paul Claudel: essai de phénoménologie littéraire.* Geneva: Droz, 1955.

Mondor, Henri. *Claudel plus intime.* Paris: Gallimard, 1960.

Perche, Louis. *Paul Claudel.* Paris: Seghers, 1948.

Raymond, Marcel. *De Baudelaire au surréalisme.* Nouvelle édition revue et remaniée. Paris: Corti, 1947.

Rimbaud, Arthur. *Oeuvres complètes. Texte établi et annoté par Rolland de Renéville et Jules Mouquet.* Paris: Gallimard, 1954.

Rivière, Jacques. *Etudes.* 9th ed. Paris: Gallimard, 1924.

Jacques Rivière et Alain-Fournier: Correspondance (1905-1914). 4 vols. Paris: Gallimard, 1926-1928.

Rivière, Jacques. *Rimbaud.* Paris: Kra, 1930.

Ryan, Mary. *Introduction to Paul Claudel.* Oxford: Cork University Press, 1951.

Rywalski, P. Pascal. *Claudel et la Bible*. Porrentruy: Editions des Portes de France, 1948.

Simon, Pierre-Henri. "La Divine tragi-comédie de Claudel," *Théâtre et Destin: la signification de la renaissance dramatique en France au XXᵉ siécle*. Paris: Armand Colin, 1959, pp. 39-62.

Starkie, Enid. *Arthur Rimbaud*. 3rd ed. London: Faber and Faber, 1961.

Weber, Jean-Paul. "Paul Claudel," *Genèse de l'oeuvre poétique*. Paris: Gallimard, 1960, pp. 338-387.

INDEX